"My good friend R. T. Kendall delivers a clear and compelling call to the church for repentance and righteousness that is desperately needed. To a generation stumbling in the darkness, *Prophetic Integrity* is biblical light from a pastor and scholar's heart which addresses the nature of God and how we can know and trust him. Read this book and discover a path forward to unite and ignite Christians and churches as we seek to fulfill the mission of Christ until he comes."

—DR. JACK GRAHAM, pastor, Prestonwood
Baptist Church, Plano, Texas

"Dr. Kendall has penned a very insightful treatise on the biblical prophetic, detailing its highest and best use. His decades-long experience with its proper deployment is invaluable to the discussion regarding how we position ourselves to hear God speak today. A necessary read."

—BRETT FULLER, pastor, Grace Covenant Church, Chantilly,
Virginia and Washington Commanders chaplain

"One of the final signs of impending judgment on a nation is the rise of false prophetic voices claiming to speak for God. Their words often contradict Scripture, while at the same time offering a nonexistent future of uninterrupted bliss. Do we have the courage to face this issue in our times? Can we correct our present course? Is there hope for today's prophetic movement? R. T. Kendall's book on our present condition offers hope. Yet it is hope based on a true self-evaluation and a humility of heart. The true prophet is not afraid of correction, but will welcome it. His desire is to honor Christ at all costs. Even though the false will always be with us, the true prophetic voices will put their babbling to shame, as has been the case throughout biblical history."

—CARTER CONLON, former pastor, Times
Square Church, New York City

T0051233

"R. T. Kendall has done it again! Yes, in his informative and timely book *Prophetic Integrity* he has managed to capture the twenty-first century's outlook about the wonderful gifts of the Holy Spirit, especially prophecy. I can say without hesitation, 'Be open to reading this book with an open mind and allow yourself the opportunity to learn whatever the Lord wants you to learn.' R. T. expounds the truths of the Word of God and expresses the necessity of allowing the gifts of the Holy Spirit to flow together with integrity while being openly transparent in all his teaching. Do you want to experience God 100 percent? *Prophetic Integrity* will give you the keys to achieving this. It will change your thinking, challenge your views, and give you much to chew on and digest!"

—MARILYN HICKEY, founder and president
of Marilyn Hickey Ministries

"In the times we live in, I cannot imagine a more qualified voice than that of R. T. Kendall to speak to the subject of prophetic integrity. From televangelists to conventions, from media preachers to conventions, and from cessationists to toll-free 800 numbers where you can get a personal prophecy on the spot, there is pervasive and embedded misinformation about biblical prophecy. Dr. Kendall has an Oxford doctorate, massive experience in a world pulpit at Westminster Chapel, and some of the most published material from a pastor/theologian of this era; no one is more qualified to speak to this issue than him. This book will clarify your thinking, give fresh impetus to genuine prophecy, and produce freedom in your church."

—JOEL C. GREGORY, holder of the George W. Truett Endowed Chair
of Preaching and Evangelism, director of the Kyle Lake Center
for Effective Preaching, George W. Truett Theological Seminary

"I count it a privilege to know Dr. Kendall as a dear friend, as one who walks the talk and whose longing has been to honour his God and to see his church revived and blessed. The spirit in which he has written about faulty theologies is consistently eirenic, with an evident heart-heavy burden for the church, for the truth, and for biblical purity and integrity of living. In this day of flaccid compromise where the world has destructively infiltrated the church rather than the church infiltrating the world, this book is both needed and intensely relevant."

—REV. DAVID COHEN, former general director of Scripture Union, UK, and founding director of Moringa Associates, Australia

"I have cried over the state of the prophetic movement—we are supposed to represent God, but we have been proven to represent party lines and opinions; we are supposed to be ones who stand before God, but we have sold ourselves to stand in front of men. May a standard be raised, and may the fame of God be restored in and through the church. May prophetic people remember that we have merely been given one of the tools that should be used in the one commission given to the church—to make disciples of Jesus Christ!"

—JOHN E. THOMAS, Streams Ministries

"If ever there was a day for prophets to 'stand before the Lord,' as Elijah did, it is today. Prophets cannot shortcut this privilege—and when they do, confusion and compromise occur. In the world of chaos and bewilderment that we live in, the word of the prophets is needed with humility, clarity, preciseness, and integrity. R. T.'s book is a good wake-up call for us all to be men and women of the secret place."

—GRANT BREWSTER, pastor, Island Church, Bainbridge Island, Washington

"*Prophetic Integrity* is timely, inspiring, and very practical. It is a much-needed book in this hour—even a godly wake-up call for many who value the prophetic ministry. R. T. combines biblical scholarship, practical application, and godly inspiration with his many years of rich ministry experience to give the body of Christ this gift of wisdom that will enrich many lives."

—MIKE BICKLE, International House of Prayer, Kansas City, Missouri

"The prophetic movement is facing a crisis of credibility across the United States and around the world. Faith in prophets and prophecy has reached a low ebb in the body of Christ—and in the world we are called to serve—as it has been battered by a plethora of unjudged and unfulfilled prophecies. R. T. Kendall, a gifted theologian, has pastored and counseled some of the leading prophetic voices in our generation, and there is no one more apt to diagnose and provide a cure for the intrinsic problems affecting prophetic integrity around the world."

—JIM LAFFOON, Every Nation Churches

PROPHETIC INTEGRITY

PROPHETIC INTEGRITY

Aligning Our Words with God's Word

R. T. KENDALL

THOMAS NELSON
Since 1798

ISBN 978-0-310-13441-1 (softcover)
ISBN 978-0-310-13443-5 (audiobook)
ISBN 978-0-310-13442-8 (eBook)

Printed in the United States of America

22 23 24 25 26 27 28 29 30 /TRM/ 13 12 11 10 9 8 7 6 5 4 3 2 1

To Alyn and A. J.

CONTENTS

FOREWORD

Just like the man, R. T. Kendall, so also his new book: both are full of wonderful surprises. But before I talk about the book, allow me a quick word about the man, who is still going strong at the age of eighty-six (as of this writing), full of conviction, full of courage, and full of curiosity. He continues his pursuit of the truth wherever it leads, combining the acumen of a theologian holding a D. Phil. from Oxford University with the spiritual openness of a charismatic who has traveled widely in prophetic circles. And it is that man who has produced this provocative and timely book.

To be perfectly candid, though, when R. T. asked me to consider writing this foreword, I accepted at once, knowing that we shared some of the same concerns about contemporary prophetic abuses and that we also shared a mutual jealousy for the honor of the Lord and the health of his Body. We are also men who are devoted to both the Word and the Spirit. And so I assumed I'd be saying "Amen" on page after page, thinking to myself as I read, "That's exactly what I would have written too." It turns out that I got more than I was expecting.

Little did I know that I'd be reading whole chapters discussing the glory of God and the God of glory. Or that we would be

delving into the serious theological error known as open theism. Or that I'd be learning about R. T.'s meetings with Yasser
Arafat. And Yogi Berra. Or that I'd hear R. T. talking about the
"thousands" of mistakes he has made over the years in terms
of properly delivering what he heard from the Lord. Talk about
surprises!

There was also the amusing story of R. T.'s private meeting
with an alleged prophet whom he thought might be of the devil.
Consequently, R. T. was secretly pleading for the blood of Jesus
to protect him—only to have that prophet tell him exactly what
he had been praying in his mind! But R. T. will share this story
in one breath, only to talk about being mentored by D. Martyn
Lloyd-Jones, his noteworthy predecessor at Westminster
Chapel, in the next breath.

There were also many, excellent nuggets on page after
page, including R. T.'s prediction of a coming Great Awakening
in which, as expressed by a colleague, "those who come to
hear will see and those who come to see will hear." R. T. also
described God's glory as "the dignity of his will" (something I
had never heard before).

There were also many probing questions, such as "Do you
suppose it matters to God if we focus on politics more than the
reason Jesus died on the cross? Are we more interested in who
is president than we are in seeing people coming to the Lord
Jesus Christ in faith? Are we more interested in preserving our
comfortable way of living than in protecting the honor and
glory of God?"

And this: "What matters to God? Is not his honor and purpose the issue that transcends all others? Moreover, is it possible
that God has taken his hand off America?"

As for the most controversial aspects of R. T.'s book, I would place these two at the top of the list: first, his conviction that the current charismatic movement is an Ishmael rather than an Isaac, despite the good that has come through it and despite the genuine operation of the spiritual gifts; and, second, that we should never say "God told me" (or the like), since to do so is to take God's name in vain and to violate the command of Jesus to let our yes be yes and our no be no. Is R. T. correct? If so, then Agabus misspoke in the New Testament when he used the formula "the Holy Spirit says" in Acts 21. (According to R. T., Agabus *was* mistaken to speak that way.)

Thus, in R. T.'s view, when we say, "The Lord told me," we are "misusing the name of the Lord" and we are "name-dropping." Indeed, he argues, "No matter how deeply one feels that he or she has a word from the Lord, there is *no need to make this claim*. One should let the other person see for himself or herself that it is from the Lord!" Is he correct?

And what of R. T.'s distinction between God's promise and God's oath? And of his exhortation that we hear an oath from God before we speak on his behalf with absolute certainty? And of the importance of understanding God's sovereignty when it comes to prophetic ministry? And of the fact that the Lord would confide in us more if we learned to keep his secrets?

These are some of the questions you will get to answer for yourself as you read the pages that follow—pages that will stimulate you to dig deeper as much as they edify and inform you. For me, personally, reading this book has not only heightened my desire to be a faithful witness to the message of the Lord. It has also provoked me to rethink some issues I had previously considered and to think for the first time about others that I never considered before. For this, I stand in debt to my esteemed, elder colleague. I believe you will feel the same as you read *Prophetic Integrity* for yourself.

Dr. Michael L. Brown
Host of the Line of Fire radio broadcast; author
of *Playing with Holy Fire: A Wake-Up Call to
the Pentecostal-Charismatic Church.*

SPECIAL RECOMMENDATION
BY CARTER CONLON

*"I have heard what the prophets have said who
prophesy lies in My name, saying, 'I have dreamed, I
have dreamed!' How long will this be in the heart of the
prophets who prophesy lies? Indeed they are prophets of
the deceit of their own heart."*

—Jeremiah 23:25–26 NKJV

One of the final signs of impending judgment on a nation
is the rise of false prophetic voices claiming to speak for
God. Their words often contradict Scripture, while at the same
time offering a nonexistent future of uninterrupted bliss. Do we
have the courage to face this issue in our times? Can we correct
our present course? Is there hope for today's prophetic movement? R. T. Kendall's book on our present condition offers hope.
Yet it is hope based on a true self-evaluation and a humility of
heart. The true prophet is not afraid of correction, but will welcome it. His desire is to honor Christ, at all costs. Even though
the false will always be with us, the true prophetic voices will

put their babbling to shame, as has been the case throughout biblical history.

> "I have not sent these prophets, yet they ran.
> I have not spoken to them, yet they prophesied.
> But if they had stood in My counsel,
> And had caused My people to hear My words,
> Then they would have turned them from their
>   evil way
> And from the evil of their doings."
>   —JEREMIAH 23:21–22 NKJV

Carter Conlon, former pastor,
Times Square Church, New York City

PREFACE

In this book I appoint myself as a peacemaker. I address both charismatic churches and evangelical churches. The issue is not merely about prophetic people getting it wrong. Non-charismatic churches have their own similar disappointments and prejudices. As a peacemaker I may be resented for trying to get people to listen to each other.

This book is about God and his attributes—whether God is all-powerful, all-knowing of the future, and sovereign. I write as simply as I know how. And my aim is to honor the God of the Bible and to show he does not change (Mal. 3:6).

I am sorry that a book like this is needed. I am on bended knee praying that it will be a wake-up call to Christians everywhere. I want this book to make a difference for lasting good.

I am very grateful to Alyn Jones, the senior associate pastor of Grace Center in Franklin, Tennessee for his shrewd criticisms regarding this book. He graciously read the original manuscript and helped me beyond measure with his suggestions. This does not mean he will agree with everything I wrote, but to show my thanks I dedicate this book to him and his lovely wife A. J. (Yes, she goes by her initials too.)

I am indebted to my British friend, Dr. Graham Ferguson Lacey, for initially suggesting I write this book and then pleading with me to undertake the task while I waited for someone else to do it. I gave in, and the book you now are reading is the result.

I also want to thank Stan Gundry, senior vice president and publisher of Zondervan Reflective, Zondervan Academic, and Study Resources, for recommending that I publish this with Thomas Nelson. I particularly appreciate my new editor, Dale Williams, for his advice. He has been terrific to work with and has wonderfully helped me, exceeding my greatest expectations. I must warmly thank Daniel Saxton for showing needed changes in my manuscript after I wrongly thought it was ready. HarperCollins Christian Publishing has the best editors under the sun! Finally, I want to express gratitude to Emily Voss for her pleasant and helpful assistance in finalizing this book for publication.

My deepest thanks, however, go to my wife Louise—my best friend and critic, known to some of my friends as Lady Solomon for her wisdom.

R. T. Kendall
Nashville, Tennessee

INTRODUCTION

American Christianity is under a cloud. A bomb of incalculable proportions has recently inflicted bedeviling damage upon a large section of the church in the United States: gross misjudgment among many charismatic Christians and gross immorality by a famous evangelical apologist.

Are you one of those who confidently predicted that Donald Trump would serve a second term as president of the United States? Was this because God told you that he would be reelected?

Are you still in shock over the sex scandal regarding the late apologist Ravi Zacharias? How could a man with his intellect and caliber, whose memorial service included a moving address by former Vice President Mike Pence, have lived a double life?

In the United Kingdom, where Louise and I have spent thirty-five years, the charismatic movement is mainstream. For example, Justin Welby, the archbishop of Canterbury, is a well-known charismatic. In the United States, however, the charismatic movement is often regarded as the lunatic fringe. A bomb of incalculable proportions has fallen in America and exploded on noncharismatic evangelicals and charismatics.

The charismatic side was bedeviled by the embarrassing failure of prophetic people who unashamedly and unanimously proclaimed in God's name that Donald Trump would serve a second consecutive term as president of the United States.

Doesn't it make sense that there should be consequences for misleading people? If a surgeon makes a mistake while operating on a child, an in-depth medical investigation would follow. If a pilot misjudges a landing and crashes a plane, the Federal Aviation Authority launches an immediate inquiry. If a judge makes a mistake, a higher court reviews the matter on appeal. A prophet in the United States makes a prediction, the outcome of which has implications for the whole world—and gets it wrong. What happens? Absolutely nothing.

Why does this matter? After all, a prophecy that got it wrong about the future of American leadership is not about the death of a child, or dozens dying on a runway, or somebody being denied justice. Who cares? *It matters if we take the Bible seriously.* Although Holy Scripture allows for prophets to be touched by the frailty of humanity, it does not allow for a cavalier attitude in which those who believe they have the prophetic gift can then say "Thus says the Lord" or "God told me" without either scrutiny or consequence. And that is so for a very good reason. When a prophet claims to speak with the voice of *Yahweh*, the God of the whole earth, God's name is at stake.

And because God's name is at stake, genuine prophets dare not prophesy according to their own personal opinion or wishes. Biblical prophets, after all, often went against their own interests. The Bible says that God reveals his secrets to those who fear him (Ps. 25:14 KJV). The fear of God transcends a true prophet's desire for immediate vindication.

The last thing I want to do is to point the finger at charismatics or evangelicals. I head the list of those who have fallen prey to the undesirable habit of saying, "God told me," and am guilty of nearly all the shortcomings I talk about in this book. My ardent prayer as I write this book is that I will speak in love and with unfeigned sympathy and compassion toward both evangelicals and charismatics.

An understanding of my background may prove helpful. I have a reputation of being a Reformed charismatic. Theologically, I am on the side of those who adhere to the doctrines of grace in historic Calvinism. I am also on the side of those who believe in the gifts of the Holy Spirit such as prophecy, healing, miracles, and speaking in tongues.

I admit to a grandiose purpose in writing this book. I hope to accomplish two things: First, I hope to succeed in getting charismatics generally and prophetic people particularly to accept needed correction. Second, I hope to succeed in causing evangelicals not only to regard charismatics with less prejudice but be willing to ask God to make them more open to the "immediate and direct" witness of the Holy Spirit. Although the late Luis Palau once said, "America is the toughest nation in the world to get denominations to work together," I am thankfully not trying to get denominations together. I only appeal to you, the reader, to consider the theological issues I pose in this book.

Here at the very beginning of this book, I want to ask some questions.

Are you a charismatic? Were you fully convinced that Donald Trump would serve another four years in the White House? Why were you convinced? Are you a prophet? Did you prophesy that Joe Biden would be the next president? If not, why not? After all, he was inaugurated president on January 20, 2021. Do you believe God knew that he would be the next president?

Or are you one who insisted that Joe Biden in fact lost the election because the Democrats stole the election? Are you claiming that Donald Trump actually won the election—insisting that your prediction was right all along?

Are you an evangelical? Is it possible that your feelings regarding political issues have become your most ardent concern? Have you allowed your love for America and our cherished traditions to become your first love? Has a preoccupation with politics replaced what should be your first love, namely, the truth about the spread of the gospel of Jesus Christ?

Ravi Zacharias was one of the most respected Christian apologists of our generation. I never knew anyone like him. He was extraordinary. So gifted. A true genius, a mind that comes along once in a century. And yet the stories that followed his death were confirmed by all who investigated the rumors and have destroyed his credibility. Christian bookshops all over America have removed his books from their shelves.

Never in my lifetime have I seen such a catastrophe afflicting the Christian church.

I personally knew Ravi Zacharias. In 2004, he kindly accepted my invitation to join me in Israel to meet with Israeli and Palestinian leaders. In my eyes, there was never a man more godly than Ravi. In retrospect, one incident with him still haunts me, in which he resorted to the "God told me" way of speaking. On the morning we planned to drive to Ramallah, Ravi shared something like this with Canon Andrew White (the archbishop of Canterbury's former envoy to the Middle East) and me: "The Lord told me in a dream last night that I should not meet Yasser Arafat." This was strange, since that meeting was one of the main reasons he had come to Israel with me. I was perplexed, if not embarrassed, since I was responsible for his visit, but despite my disappointment I did go to Ramallah without Ravi. This sudden change of mind in Ravi shows that from the least-known Christian to the most famous many fall prey to the "God told me" syndrome. And yet the disclosure of Ravi's dissolute private life has given the world all the ammunition it has wanted to reject orthodox Christianity.

I have been in the ministry for over sixty-five years. I have spoken to many denominations, and I know firsthand how charismatics and evangelicals think. I know what makes them "tick." In this book I will share what I know that will address the "God told me" habit that is a common way of speaking for many Christians. I admit that I myself have all too often been guilty of claiming this. It is a hard habit to break.

I want to ask, what is it that matters to God? Is his honor and purpose not the issue that transcends all others? Moreover, is it possible that God has taken his hand off America?

Chapter 1

MY ENCOUNTER WITH THE PROPHETIC

And he gave the apostles, the prophets, the evangelists, the shepherds and teachers, to equip the saints for the work of ministry, for building up the body of Christ, until we all attain to the unity of the faith and of the knowledge of the Son of God, to mature manhood, to the measure of the stature of the fullness of Christ, so that we may no longer be children, tossed to and fro by the waves and carried about by every wind of doctrine, by human cunning, by craftiness in deceitful schemes.

—EPHESIANS 4:11–14

Do not despise prophecies, but test everything; hold fast what is good.

—1 THESSALONIANS 5:20–21

At first we might expect that New Testament prophets
would be like the Old Testament prophets. But when we
look through the New Testament itself this does not seem
to be the case.

—WAYNE GRUDEM

I have been a preacher for a long time. However, my encounter with the *prophetic* only happened after I had already been in ministry for thirty-five years. Prophetic ministry was a new world for me—a world of the good, the bad, and the ugly.

Before my encounter, prophecy meant something different during the early days of my ministry. The church I was raised in emphasized the signs of the times, the Antichrist, the secret rapture of the church, the great tribulation, and the book of Revelation. Prophecy was associated with "the last days," not types of people.

During my college years, I took a course on the New Testament at Trevecca Nazarene College (now University) and felt sure that I understood the book of Revelation. I will never forget the day when my professor asked, "Next week we come to the book of Revelation. I'm not sure I understand this book. Is there anyone here who does?" My hand shot up like a Polaris missile. "Oh, brother Kendall, how would you like to teach the book of Revelation?" Of course, I agreed and taught the class what I knew a week later. I expounded on the pretribulation rapture, the man of sin, and the millennium. I thought I had done a brilliant job and couldn't wait for the praise of my classmates and professor. However, one fellow student simply asked me whether I always held my mouth open while speaking. My professor thanked me kindly but said, "You might be right, but who knows?" It was a humiliating experience, but I was still fixated on last days prophecy.

A few years later, in the late 1950s, I preached on eschatological prophecy at my church in Palmer, Tennessee. My father was there, and I was eager to hear what he thought. It took him more than an hour to share his thoughts with me. "Son," he suggested, "let me give you a word that came from the man I named you after, Dr. R. T. Williams. He said, 'Young men, stay away from the subject of prophecy. Let the old men do that. That way they won't be around to see their mistakes.'" Consequently, many years passed before I spoke again about prophecy or the signs of the times.

My chief mentor, Dr. Martyn Lloyd-Jones, also said that the Bible was not given to replace the revelatory gift of prophecy but to correct abuses. This helped me understand that prophecy was direct communication from God that may refer to the past, present, or future, and that testing such communication was part of the ministry.

Fast forward to the early 1990s, when I discovered a new meaning for prophecy and the prophetic. This season changed my life and ministry.

The Kansas City Prophets

The book *Some Said It Thundered*, written by Anglican bishop David Pitches, was a bestseller in the United Kingdom during the early 1990s. This book introduced me and many others around the world to the "Kansas City Prophets." Several prophetic men were featured, especially Paul Cain (1929–2019),

Bob Jones (1930–2014), and John Paul Jackson (1950–2015). These men went to heaven in recent years. James Goll and Larry Randolph, friends of mine now living in the Nashville area, were also mentioned. All these men were the leading speakers at a major prophetic conference in Kansas City, so Bishop Pitches gave them the nickname "Kansas City Prophets."

I got to know all five of these Kansas City Prophets, especially Paul Cain and John Paul Jackson. Paul Cain was regarded as the most spectacular. He was said to be a protégé of William Branham (1909–1965), a prophet I heard in Parkersburg, West Virginia, in 1957. My dad said that at one point Branham looked in his direction and gave an encouraging prophetic word, which he hoped applied to me. What made Branham impressive was how he called out the names of people with a high level of accuracy. He also prayed for sick people. However, there was an odd side to Branham's ministry: he demanded that people answer "Yes" to his question, "Do you believe I am God's prophet?" After praying for several people, he would lose strength, fall backward, and get carried off the platform. Paul Cain repeatedly said that his own gift was minute compared to that of William Branham.

Branham's prophetic ministry was a forerunner to the Kansas City Prophets. As far as I know, he was the first prophet to publicly call people out and pray for them to be healed. His visions were extraordinary; for example, Paul Cain told me that one morning at breakfast Branham described Paul's dream from the previous night in great detail.

At the time, I was uneasy with the whole idea of prophetic ministry. The prophets were scheduled to visit a prominent Anglican church in London, and I was probably jealous that they were not coming to my church. I thought that if God was going to visit London in an unusual way, Westminster Chapel would have been better than an Anglican church. At my church, we did have days of prayer and fasting. I once risked my reputation by inviting Arthur Blessitt, the man who has carried a cross around the world, to preach in my pulpit, which nearly got me fired. In my unconscious self-righteousness I felt that we at Westminster Chapel deserved to have God honor us more than the Church of England, which was filled with aristocratic people and their posh accents!

But I was wrong.

Bob Jones

Word got out that I was willing to meet some prophetic men. John Wimber (1934–1997), pastor of the Anaheim Vineyard and leader of the Vineyard movement, kindly flew Louise and me to Anaheim, California. At breakfast in our hotel, Bob Jones sat across the table from me. Since I knew he was one of the prophets, I was nervous and cautious, beginning to earnestly pray in my heart, "Jesus, cover me with your blood." "Jesus, cover me with your blood." "Jesus, cover me with your blood." As I prayed these words, Bob smiled and said, "Jesus, cover me with your blood." Then he looked at me and continued, "It's good that you prayed that." Oh dear, I thought. This man knows my very thoughts. It embarrassed me that Bob knew I was unsure of his prophetic gift. But what could I say?

Not all prophets read minds! But some, like it or not, have this gift.

What I initially knew about Bob Jones came through secondhand stories from Ricky Skaggs and Mike Bickle, the latter being the pastor and founder of the International House of Prayer in Kansas City. But I was able to personally experience Bob's ministry myself, especially when he spoke some comforting words that helped me get through a scary time. I had open heart surgery in Nashville in 2008, and Ricky brought Bob to my bedside the day after my surgery. While the anesthetic wore off, Bob stood by me and prophesied for at least an hour. I remember him saying that he saw me as a "canopy" and under the canopy were people of different perspectives, such as Word people and Spirit people. This meant a lot to me.

I will not tell the stories I heard about Bob from Mike and Ricky. These stories will come out in a matter of time once Bob's biography gets written. However, they were quite extraordinary and comparable to what people told about Paul Cain.

Paul Cain

Before the Kansas City Prophets came to London, Paul Cain spoke prophetically to John Wimber and predicted that revival would come to London in 1990. The word spread. It was noised abroad that Paul Cain's predictions always came to pass. John Wimber once told me that Paul had spoken prophetic words over a hundred and fifty families in his church in California and never got anything wrong.

The more I heard about Paul Cain, the more I wanted to meet him—and many others felt the same way. I felt like I had won the lottery when a friend of mine gave me Paul's phone number. In November 1990 Paul and I met for lunch at a hotel near Tower Bridge in London, and my close friend Lyndon Bowring joined us.

I learned afterward that John Wimber had run into Reed Grafke, Paul's assistant, and said, "Reed, there is someone I want Paul to meet—R. T. Kendall."

Reed replied, "They are having lunch right now." When John realized Paul and I were together, he and Reed prayed in the parking lot for our meeting.

As eager as I was to meet Paul, I still brought a grave skepticism to our encounter. That threw him off. He told me later that he always felt uncomfortable when someone was unsure of him. But then he said to me, "When I heard your name, even though I had never heard of you, I was so excited. It has been years since I felt so excited to meet someone." I was flattered—but later on I learned that he said the same thing to others.

As we ate lunch together, Paul shared things about my life that he could not have known. He had insight into my psychology, calling me a "maverick" but recognizing that I longed for "vindication." He also gave me a word about a mental block I had. These insights softened me toward him. I cannot say whether this came from the Holy Spirit or from flattery, but I was hooked within an hour or so.

A few days after our lunch meeting, Paul came to our School of Theology at Westminster Chapel. After I finished teaching, I introduced him and asked him to speak to the congregation, as he was unknown to most of the members. His word to us was this: "Seek God's face, not his hand." He meant we should desire to know God for his own sake rather than to ask him to do things for us. Like me, the congregation was impressed.

After the School of Theology session, Paul and I went out for a meal at the Aberdeen Steak House on Victoria Street. As we ate, I said to him, "Paul, you need my theology. And I need your power."

"You have a deal," he replied.

The Word and Spirit concept, as it has become known, was planted in that meeting. That concept grew into a conference that stressed both the importance of the Word of God and the personal experience of the Holy Spirit. I shall say more about this later.

A few months later, Paul phoned me out of the blue to say he would be in London the following day. He lived in Dallas, Texas, and claimed the Lord had spoken to him, "Go to London immediately." He wanted to hear me preach and to grasp my Reformed theology, which was totally new to him. We found a place for him to stay across the street from the Chapel. Call it coincidence or providence that he chose this time to visit, because I was solidly booked to preach in various places in England for the subsequent two weeks. Since it was unusual for me to be booked to preach so often, I took this as a sign of God's seal on our relationship. Paul listened to me preach almost every night somewhere in England, getting a good dose of my theology. I believed I was being led to sort him out! Or was I?

Despite the wonderful connection I had made with Paul, his prophecy about revival coming to London in 1990 did not happen. We were disappointed. Were we misled by the word that Paul gave about London? Did Paul get this wrong? When I asked him about the prophecy, he got defensive: "I said there would be 'tokens' of revival." But we had expected much more than tokens of revival. I was amazed by the way Paul exercised prophetic ministry but not by the way he avoided correction. This always worried me.

In October 1992, Paul and I held our first Word and Spirit conference at the Wembley Conference Centre in London. Lyndon Bowring chaired the meeting, and Graham Kendrick wrote a hymn stressing Word and Spirit, "Jesus Restore to Us Again." Some 2,500 people, mostly charismatics, were present. That was a powerful preaching experience for me; I will say more about what I taught that day in the chapter entitled "Word and Spirit."

My family grew close to Paul; he even spent vacations with us in Key Largo, Florida. I will never forget a conversation I had with him at my favorite fishing spot when the bonefish did not seem to be nearby. I told Paul that I had been praying for a clear witness of the Holy Spirit so that I would truly be linked with him. However, Paul was hurt that I wasn't sure, since he had previously indicated that he and I were to have a Word and Spirit ministry together. Yes, I was excited about this—but I wanted to be sure. "Now isn't this something?" Paul commented. "Everyone on the planet would give the world to be with me, and here you are not even sure we should be together." Paul's prophetic gift was so powerful that he could be mistaken for Elijah or Elisha. The fact that Paul wanted to be linked with me made me so happy, and the thought that God wanted this gave me even greater assurance that I was in his will. Nevertheless, for some reason the clarity I was looking for was withheld from me.

One never knew when Paul's prophetic gift would "kick in." Forgive me for using that term; I learned many phrases that describe prophetic activity. Paul would suddenly say or do something that surprised us. That is why I describe his gifting in this way.

Paul loved the TV show *Columbo*. I remember watching *Columbo* with Paul one night, when the phone rang. Our friend Benjamin Chan had gone to pick up dinner and was calling to ask if Paul liked Chinese food. "That man will make you a good deacon," Paul interrupted. "He had a son, William, which is not a very Chinese name, who is now in heaven because he died of a hole in his heart. But he and his wife now have a son, Wing Yung, which is a Chinese name." That spontaneous outburst by Paul happened in seconds, and it was remarkable because Paul did not know that I had visited Benjamin, his wife Fong Hah Chan, and their son William—who was gravely ill with a hole in his heart. I had cried as I held William's little warm body in my arms minutes after he died. Fong Hah's chief concern was that little William was in heaven, and I had assured her that he was. I phoned Benjamin back and told him that the assurance about William being in heaven, which he and Fong Hah had prayed for, had been confirmed by Paul. Paul's word transcended my word to them while we were watching *Columbo*!

If one is looking for the purpose of a prophetic gift, I think the story in the preceding paragraph answers this. Benjamin indeed became a deacon at Westminster Chapel two years later, and was one of my most faithful supporters. A few years ago, after my retirement, I returned to Westminster Chapel as a visiting preacher and Benjamin's son Wing Yung came to Christ under my ministry. Paul had seen something long before these events occurred.

As I said a moment ago, Paul had the most extraordinary

prophetic gift of any I have met. Everybody wanted to listen to him. They were not there for his preaching (which was mediocre) but for his uncanny accuracy in calling out people publicly. He would spontaneously share details about the called-out person that only he or she knew. For example, I watched a lady named Elizabeth, whom I knew well, get transformed by Paul's direct word to her in the middle of one of his sermons. Nearly all whom I talked to about Paul's ministry compared him to Elijah. To me, however, he ministered more like Elisha in 2 Kings.

This is not a biography about Paul Cain. Someone does need to write about his life and gift. But I am sharing these stories about Paul because they help us understand how prophets use their gift today. Paul's prophetic style including predictions, calling people's names out in services for healing, and having questionable theology can also be seen in today's prophets.

Paul asked if he could become a member of Westminster Chapel. Because he lived in Texas, I said no. Paul countered me by saying that if Billy Graham could live in North Carolina and be a member of First Baptist Church in Dallas, why could he not be a member of Westminster Chapel? I said he would have to attend the Chapel for six months before he could apply. "What if I listen to six months of your tapes?" he asked, and then added, "More than anything I have wanted in my life, I want to be a member of Westminster Chapel." Maybe he knew that people thought he had a reputation of being theologically shallow and hoped that being under my ministry would help his reputation. In any case, I brought Paul's request to the Chapel and they unanimously voted to let him be a member. When I phoned Paul to give him the news that he had been voted in, he replied, "Now I can say I am a Reformed minister."

I still believe God led me to see the prophetic as I did, and thank him for this. I believe in the value of solid and sound prophetic ministry, and I believe God uses the prophetic today. But I had to adjust to the realization that most prophetic men I got to know were not the slightest bit theological. This was hard for me to take. It was as if their gift was disconnected from their doctrine.

Reader, you may be disappointed, if not shocked, that I still believe in prophetic ministry after my friendship with Paul and the more recent debacle with the charismatic prophets' rendezvous with American politics. It is enough to make one categorically dismiss the entire idea, but I will say more.

Paul did admit to me that his theology was about one inch deep. It saddened me to learn that he had never read the Bible all the way through. I persuaded him to begin following the Robert Murray M'Cheyne Bible reading plan, but he didn't keep it up. Paul was quite intelligent, but was no intellectual. I liked Paul a lot. He and his assistant Reed were great fun, and we laughed a lot together. They loved my wife Louise's cooking and ate her popcorn whenever they could. One evening Paul put his hand on the man our daughter Melissa was then dating. The man's neck pain was instantly healed from a prior injury. Later on, when Melissa wandered from the Lord, Louise and I were very burdened, so we asked Paul, "Will she be okay?" He replied, "You will have to let her go. It will be a wait. But she will be back." Paul loved puns. *Wait* in this case could have been spelled *weight*, for this was very heavy for us. Melissa did come back years later. She is now happily married and lives near us.

Paul once told me an extraordinary story about guest preaching in Oklahoma when he was very young. While he was preaching, a lady began speaking in tongues. Paul asked the lady, "Please stop. You are out of order." But she continued. He pleaded with her a second time. After a third warning Paul said, "Sister, you are not in the Spirit. Please stop. If you don't, I will reveal what I know about you." She still continued speaking in tongues. Then, according to reports, Paul interrupted: "You are having an affair with the man sitting over here. In fact, you have plans to go out with this man this very night. He is leaving his wife for you." Silence fell upon the room.

After this revelatory word, the church's pastor came up to Paul after the revelatory word and told him that he was ending the meeting. The reason the pastor gave was that people were not being converted. "That is not why you are closing the meeting," Paul replied. "You are closing down the meeting because the adulterous man I referred to tonight has promised you a million dollars for your new church building."

"That's a lie," retorted the pastor.

"Oh, I wish you had not said that," Paul responded. "You will not be alive to preach in your new building."

The pastor then replied, "Paul, please take that back, and I will have you back here later."

Paul got a phone call from a member of that church two years later. On the day of the dedication of the new church building, the pastor walked into the vestibule and fell dead from a heart attack.

After Paul told me this story, he continued, "That was when I was young. I decided I would stop calling out people for their sin and only say things that would encourage people." Several times since then, I wondered whether Paul's decision to say only nice things caused the Spirit to lift from his ministry.

13

It is important for me to repeat that I still believe in the prophetic. We all make mistakes. If you are not a charismatic, please don't dig in your heels and refuse to see at least some merit in what I hold to. This isn't black or white. If you are a charismatic, please don't be defensive but be open to some correction.

The last time Paul preached for us at Westminster Chapel, he compared worship to the mist and vapor that rises from earth to form clouds that bring rain. He said that our worship was like the hydrological cycle—it rises to heaven and brings down the blessing of the Holy Spirit. That sermon was life-changing. From that moment I decided to add to my quiet time fifteen minutes of singing aloud every morning and ten minutes every evening. At first it felt funny singing aloud with Louise listening to me. Now it has gone on for twenty-five years; I do this every morning and evening. I choose hymnals, chorus books, and psalms. This pattern of personal devotions would not have happened apart from Paul Cain.

Despite the incongruities, perplexities, and disappointments I experienced with Paul, I thank God for him. And even though their loud music, their often theologically shallow praise songs, their flag waving, and their jumping up and down can make me uncomfortable, I know that charismatics love God.

For a very long time my understanding of prophecy was only eschatological, limited to the end times. Then the Kansas City Prophets changed my perspective and pulled me into the deep end with a new understanding of the prophetic ministry, creating a new world for me.

Chapter 2

THE GOOD, THE BAD, AND THE UGLY

For the gifts and the calling of God are irrevocable.

—ROMANS 11:29

"Nothing is covered up that will not be revealed,
or hidden that will not be known."

—LUKE 12:2

"Be sure your sin will find you out."

—NUMBERS 32:23

Sometimes God offends our minds in order to reveal
our hearts.

—JOHN WIMBER (1934–1997)

I served as pastor of Westminster Chapel for twenty-five years (1977–2002). The years of ministry with charismatics and prophetic people in the 1990s were thrilling, creating many ups and downs. By the spring of 2000, I began to consider retiring from Westminster Chapel. I saw no signs of the fulfillment of the great revival prophesied by Paul Cain, and I accepted the fact that it would not come while I was pastor. I began to wonder what I would do if I was not the pastor of a church. It was (and still is) too expensive for most people to live in London. I did not think anybody knew me in America. Should I move to Key Largo, Florida, and become a recluse, fishing for the rest of my days? As I despaired about what would come next I heard the words, "Your ministry in America will be to charismatics."

I was so disappointed!

I wanted to minister to evangelicals. I had gone to the right seminary and had earned the DPhil from Oxford. I knew how evangelicals thought, and I felt I had something they needed. Then another thought came to me about the Apostle Paul and his desire to reach the Jews. The Spirit had directed him to the Gentiles instead. Of course, I wasn't equating myself to the Apostle Paul or thinking that prophetic ministry was on par with Holy Scripture. But I began to take comfort as I remembered how the church had grown when the Apostle reached the Gentiles.

Notice in the previous paragraph how I described my decision process. I used language popular in charismatic circles: "a thought came to me." I couldn't tell you how much of these thoughts were my own or God's, but I was pretty sure they were nudges by the Spirit. They were not flashy, but they got my attention.

The influence of high-profile evangelists and prophets on my later life and ministry will likely show up in my memoir, if I write one. I will explain how my invitations of Arthur Blessitt and Paul Cain to Westminster Chapel made evangelicals distance themselves from me. I was deeply hurt when evangelicals turned against me, although charismatics did embrace me. In fact, my good friend and longtime publisher Steve Strang believed in me so much that he published more than thirty books of mine with Charisma House.

I am very sympathetic to charismatics. Despite my Reformed theology, I hope they will accept some correction from me because I am a charismatic as much as I am an evangelical. And my corrections come from a good place, since I have also gone through the ups and downs of prophetic ministry. The best way I can summarize my experience within the prophetic movement is by borrowing from the title of the classic Western film *The Good, the Bad and the Ugly*. Over the years, I have seen some good, some bad, and some ugly in prophetic individuals as well as in larger movements.

The Good

In January 1991, John Wimber invited me to attend a prophetic conference to meet some important people at the Anaheim Vineyard. I met Dr. Jack Deere, who had been an adamant cessationist before becoming a well-known man of the Spirit. I also met Mike Bickle, who was keen for me to meet a prophetic friend of his. Everything was strange about this meeting; before it began, I had to wait in a room that looked a lot like a doctor's waiting room. The feeling of waiting for a doctor to invite me in for a checkup did not change when my name was eventually called.

Mike introduced me to John Paul Jackson, but did not tell him my name. John Paul had never heard of me, nor had he heard of Westminster Chapel. And I only vaguely knew who he was: one of the Kansas City Prophets. John Paul began by saying this to me: "Twenty years ago was a turning point in your life." That was actually true. At the time of him saying this it had been twenty years since I had returned to finish my education at Southern Baptist Theological Seminary. As John Paul continued speaking, I had to admit that what he said was accurate. The last thing he told me was, "I see three books coming from you." Three days later, I returned to London where a Scottish publisher, Christian Focus, asked me to write three books for them. I was amazed, bewildered, and thrilled.

John Paul regarded Paul Cain as his hero, but his gift was not as sensational as Paul's. John Paul often gave prophecies based on dreams. He was most comfortable interpreting a person's dream; in fact, he was writing a book on dream interpretation when he died. One might say it was his expertise: he would interpret a person's dream and then try to lead that person to the Lord. John Paul also claimed that he had been transported to heaven three times. A word he gave to me was based on one of these heavenly visitations. As a consequence of one visitation he predicted that "the key to the next great move of God is the book of Romans, especially Romans chapter four." However, John Paul had no idea what Romans 4 was about. One of my huge disappointments with both Paul Cain and John Paul Jackson was their lack of theological-mindedness and understanding of the Bible. But I was thrilled—and still am—at the thought of Romans 4 being the key to the next great move of God; it means a return to the gospel!

In 1993 John Paul came to London, and I brought him to the pulpit at Westminster Chapel. He prophesied, "I feel a balloon that gets larger and larger and explodes and goes around the world." I did not know how to interpret that then or now. If it was a word from God, I would have to say it will be fulfilled somehow in the future. Afterward, we went to the vestry to talk. I asked John Paul if he had a word about Louise, my wife. He did, and it was astonishingly accurate. I then asked about our son T. R. He said that God would use T. R. to bring revival to Westminster Chapel. I felt disappointed and could not believe this, because at that time T. R. resided in Florida, across the Atlantic Ocean from Westminster Chapel, and was not living for the Lord. I thought John Paul had missed it entirely. I had mixed feelings about his visit. He had shared an odd prophecy that I could not interpret and spoke a word that rang true for my wife, but seemed to miss hearing God for my son.

A couple years after John Paul's visit, however, T. R. had a spiritual encounter that turned him completely around. Deacon Benjamin Chan asked me if T. R. would be interested in returning to London to work for him as a computer programmer. To our surprise, T. R. immediately came. It was not long before he gathered some young people around him and they began having prayer meetings, singing together in our apartment. Within a few weeks, the number of young people at Westminster Chapel grew in numbers and spiritual maturity. This group of young people also began praying for others that they might receive God's blessing. A guitar player among the group, Kieran Grogan, became our worship leader. His wife Beryl later became my secretary.

One Sunday night, I invited some of the young people to give their testimonies. They testified that they had been deeply touched by the Holy Spirit, and the most mature members in the Chapel were moved by their words. After the testimonies, I invited anyone who wanted to be prayed for by our young people to go to the back halls. Nearly two hundred wanted prayer. Soon afterward we began having healing services. Those who requested prayer for healing came to the front rows of the church, where they were prayed for and anointed with oil by the deacons as in James 5:14. Some were miraculously healed. That was when Westminster Chapel became a Word and Spirit church. I cannot say it was revival—but it was wonderful. And it all began with T. R., who pretty much fulfilled John Paul's prophecy.

In September 2001, John Paul visited me again in London. He prophesied that a forthcoming trip to Israel would create a close and intimate relationship with those accompanying me, which would go on for years and years. He was so right. In July 2002, Lyndon Bowring, Alan Bell, and I were unexpectedly invited to meet Yasser Arafat. Consequently, we have traveled together some fifteen times.

After I retired from Westminster Chapel in 2002, my family moved to Key Largo. John Paul visited me there and I introduced him to bonefishing. It was a privilege to get to know John Paul very well during this time, and I got to know him better than Paul Cain.

One evening in Key Largo, in the middle of our dinner with Louise, T. R., and Annette (T. R.'s wife), John Paul put his knife and fork down and said: "R. T., you will live to a ripe old age, but if you don't get in shape physically, you won't be around to enjoy it." This news shook me; I was sixty-eight, flabby and overweight. John Paul's track record in prophetic words was impressive enough to make me take him seriously. I then began daily exercises and T. R. bought me a book that changed my eating habits. I also hired a trainer. I have been doing twenty-one push-ups every day (not by Olympic standards but not bad for an old man).

John Paul Jackson went to heaven six years ago. At age eighty-six, I am thankfully in good health.

Sadly, John Paul's prophecies regarding his *own* future did not pan out. The day before he died, he was talking about his future ministry. At only sixty-five years of age, he did not believe he would die so young.

Aside from the accuracy of his prophecies over my family and myself, three things impressed me most about John Paul. First, he stressed the fact that character was much more important than one's gift. Some today emphasize the opposite, that people's gifts are more important than how they conduct their lives. Second, John Paul believed God's knowledge of the future was and is just as perfect as his knowledge about the past. John Paul believed in God's sovereignty and foreknowledge; open theism would be abhorrent to him. Third, John Paul was teachable and eager to learn.

My good experiences with John Paul show the form of prophetic ministry I am most comfortable with—a privately shared word for an individual by someone with a revelatory gift. Most of the time, however, people do not have a friend that claims to be a prophet. They instead seek out public prophesying at special church services or conferences. Public prophesying brings in the crowds! People will wait for the sermon to finish before the "main event," when the prophet stands on the stage, looks across the congregation, singles out a person, and shares a word or short message that makes the individual feel like God notices him or her in that moment. We may call this public prophesying a word of knowledge or a prophetic word, and it is always exciting to behold.

An example of thrilling public prophesying happened in Sydney, Australia, where over five thousand people attended. Paul Cain stopped in the middle of his sermon to call out a group of five people in the balcony farthest from the platform. He said: "You people on the first two rows of the far balcony—you don't know each other, you are in a cluster. All of you have diabetes, and the Lord is healing you now." Indeed, these five people did not know each other, and all of them had diabetes. A report later arrived that they all claimed to have been healed. As if that was not enough, while Paul was speaking to the cluster, another man who was a diabetic in the balcony to the right began to pray silently, "O Lord, please have Paul Cain call me out." Paul then turned and pointed to that very man, who shouted "YES!" He went to his physician the next day and was told he was no longer diabetic. When I asked Paul about that occasion in Sydney, he told me that as he called out the cluster of the five diabetics he saw a blue line. He followed this line, which led straight to the man to his right, and then called him out.

Strange? Oh, yes. But this was good, too. These people, unknown to Paul, were called out by him and reportedly healed of diabetes—they had been freed from their troublesome affliction. Paul chuckled when he told me this story, commenting that one of the men healed was a cessationist!

The Bad

In my book *Holy Fire*, I attempt to refute cessationism. Even though I believe in the ongoing presence and work of the Spirit, I admit that charismatics can be strange. One chapter in the book is called "Strange Fire." I talk about some pretty horrible and bizarre stuff among some high-profile charismatics, some of whom are on TV. You can also read about the strange stories from the ministry of George Whitefield (1714–1770), a hero among the Reformed pastors.

On one occasion, Whitefield stationed a trumpet player to sound his trumpet at a strategic point in his sermon on the second coming. When Whitefield preached that Jesus would come back at the sound of a trumpet, the trumpeter blew his instrument to suggest that Jesus was coming right then! People fell. Some screamed, believing it was too late for them to be saved. However, conversions likely happened. As a cousin of mine from Kentucky used to say, tongue in cheek, "God moves in mischievous ways his wonders to perform."

There is a lot of symbolism among the Old Testament prophets that is outside our comfort zones. It is not necessarily bad when something is strange, since God may allow things that offend our minds to reveal our hearts.

I used to preach annually at a well-known event called Spring Harvest. One year there were approximately five thousand people. A popular charismatic leader was there and called me back onto the platform with him. He prophesied to me: "Eighteen months from now, eighteen months from now, eighteen months from now Westminster Chapel will be unrecognizable." He suggested a great move of the Holy Spirit would come to us.

I loved this, of course. But it didn't happen. And worse still, people who were suspicious of prophecy left our church. In my opinion, the devil took advantage of this sad situation. The man who gave the prophecy claimed that he heard people say that Westminster Chapel had become "unrecognizable." But the implied revival never came.

Did I misunderstand the prophecy? Did our congregation think the message given applied to Westminster Chapel in a different way than how I imagined? Should the prophet be held accountable for imploring God's name before so many people?

This was a bad look.

Unfortunately, this happens more than I want to admit. What worries me is that some people believe their prophetic gift is virtually equal to Holy Scripture. This is bad—very bad. It crosses over a line. Even when a prophecy comes to pass, it is not equal to Scripture. John Paul Jackson, a man who got a lot of prophecies right, never imagined his prophecies were equal to Scripture.

One evening, my friends Rob Parsons, Lyndon Bowring, and I attended a midweek service at a church in London. An American prophet whom I had never met spoke. The three of us tried to be inconspicuous, so we sat way in the back. However, the man in charge recognized us and insisted that we sit on the front row, right in front of the speaker. When the prophet began I noticed that he kept looking at me, which made me feel awkward. I wrote a note to Lyndon, "Make me smile. This man is in bondage to me." Lyndon wrote a cheeky note (ask to see it in heaven!) that made me burst out laughing. I was embarrassed. But it set the prophet free from staring at me. He then prophesied to me, and like the prophet from the Spring Harvest event he said that a great revival would come to Westminster Chapel. I would lead a School of Miracles ministry. I would be on television programs broadcast around the world. And world leaders would come to my vestry seeking my wisdom.

A couple of days later the speaker came to see me and asked if he could speak at Westminster Chapel. Was this his motive in prophesying as he did, to get me to invite him to preach for me? Why did my laughing release him to prophesy over me? I did not allow him to preach at Westminster Chapel.

John Paul invited me to address a Prophetic Convergence Conference in Dallas several years ago. There were approximately seventy people in attendance who had a prophetic gift. I spoke on the third commandment ("You shall not misuse the name of the Lord") and explained why saying "Thus says the Lord" or "God told me" violates Jesus's application of the third commandment. I expected them all to clobber me, but to my surprise many came up to me and admitted that my word was what they needed to hear.

To say "God told me" is a habit hard to break; Paul Cain and John Paul Jackson did this all the time. Many of us have done this regardless of our theological tradition. It is bad, and we need to stop doing it.

The Ugly

In 2008 we got overwhelmed with phone calls and emails from England. People asked us, "Isn't it wonderful that revival has broken out in Florida?" Some called it "the last day ministries." Services from the revival's center, Lakeland, were telecast live all over the world through GOD TV. Never in my lifetime had I seen such an evangelistic opportunity. GOD TV even reportedly reached countries where the gospel had not been preached.

Louise and I watched the events nightly. However, Louise struggled with what she saw. "There's something wrong," she kept saying. I kept watching, wanting to believe that this was a genuine move of the Spirit.

The more I watched, the more I began to question whether this was a move of the Spirit or not. I asked myself, "If this is a Holy Spirit revival that is going into countries where the gospel had never penetrated, why doesn't the evangelist preach the gospel?" Would the gospel be preached even once, at least? I kept waiting, but the only thing I heard the evangelist say was, "words of knowledge," referring to someone's physical condition. When a specific condition was called out, people would go to the platform and the evangelist would shout out a one-word prayer: "Bam!" I had no idea whether the words of knowledge were accurate or if people were healed. There were nightly reports of people being raised from the dead in a local hospital. "If even *one* person was raised from the dead," I thought, "surely that would have made world news." However, only charismatics knew about these events.

A dozen well-known charismatic leaders went to Lakeland to endorse the Lakeland Revival and the evangelist. I too was invited, and one beloved friend begged me to join these leaders. I refused to go, saying that what was going on was "not of God." "Oh, R. T., please don't say that," my friend pleaded. A major charismatic magazine devoted an entire issue to the Lakeland Revival, asking me to write an article for it. As far as I knew, I was the only one to publicly question what was happening in

Lakeland. Some of my friends were hurt or horrified that I took such a strong stand against the so-called revival.

At one point there were as many as thirteen thousand people present, so the services had to be moved to a local stadium. Paul Cain was on the platform and spoke, claiming that the revival was the fulfillment of a vision he had years before—that there would be revival services in a large stadium. He had told me about this vision before, but I was surprised to hear him say Lakeland was its fulfillment because as I saw things, they did not even come close to the details he had shared with me.

John Paul Jackson and I stood in agreement in our belief that the Lakeland meetings were not of God. First, the gospel was never preached by the evangelist. I could not believe that God would put his seal on meetings that were telecast all over the world when the gospel of his Son who died on the cross for our sins was not preached. There were only a "word of knowledge" and "Bam!" when people were prayed for. Second, there was no conviction of sin in the services. No sense of sin existed at all. On the contrary, true revival will bring about conviction of sin. Third, when the leaders of the revival baptized, they trivialized the Holy Spirit. People were baptized "in the name of the Father, the Son, and Bam!" No one seemed to feel uneasy about this downplaying of the Trinity. No one objected. This was one of the ugliest expressions of prophetic ministry I can remember—and I have been in ministry a long time.

The charismatic leaders that asked me to join them in Lakeland prophesied a great future for the Lakeland evangelist. They used catchphrases such as, "the Spirit of God says" and "thus saith the Lord." They gathered around him and laid hands on him, stating that they "ordained" him and "commissioned" him to the world. One leader said, "We shape the course of history by partnering with you." They also prayed that "the measure of glory would increase so that Moses would no longer be considered the high watermark with the glory shone from his face."

This evangelist would be greater than Moses! I'm not making this up! You can find the video of this on YouTube, for anyone to see.

Within a month or so, the "revival" suddenly closed. The evangelist was caught in immorality that had been going on the entire time. All the prophecies proved to be wrong. My beloved friend, who had asked me to go to Lakeland, wrote me a very honest and moving apologetic letter. He did not need to do that—but he did, and I appreciated and respected him for it. Unfortunately, one of the better-known leaders who went to Lakeland and was one of those "ordaining" the evangelist later said, "I didn't actually lay my hands on him." In saying that, as John Paul put it, "He threw his fellow leaders under the bus."

For charismatics, nothing good that I know of came from the Lakeland Revival.

Again, it was so ugly.

What saddens me most is that the Lakeland meetings might have continued indefinitely had the evangelist not been caught in his adultery. The absence of gospel preaching was not a problem for the revival's attendees and listeners at the time.

How did the gift of "word of knowledge" thrive when the evangelist was living in immorality? How could the evangelist get it right? Why did some people he ministered to experience healing? How did all these wonderful things happen when the evangelist was engaged in the midst of sin and licentiousness?

Could an answer to these questions be found in Romans 11:29, which says, "For the gifts and the calling of God are irrevocable"? This could mean that the gifts may thrive even while a preacher, prophet, or evangelist lives a double life. This could explain how King Saul, *on his way to kill young David, prophesied*! The Spirit of God fell on him and he prophesied. The onlookers even asked, "Is Saul also among the prophets?" (1 Sam. 19:23–24). Figure that one out!

In 2020, dozens, if not hundreds, of prophets said that God had told them Trump would begin a second term in 2021. Did they apologize? Not that many. Thank God for the ones that did. Many of them, however—even some of my friends—are still insisting that God told them Trump actually won. Not even one of them predicted that Joe Biden would be inaugurated on January 20, 2021.

For as long as I live, I will never forget the level of disbelief and disappointment I felt when I learned about another prophet's moral failure. A very close friend I was traveling with met me at Terminal B in the Dallas/Fort Worth International Airport. We were on our way to a preaching assignment when he asked, "Have you heard about Paul?" "No," I replied. "What do you mean?" I then learned that Paul Cain was in a moral free fall. News had spread that he was secretly a practicing homosexual. That was one of the worst days of my life; I felt deceived. As the word leaked out all over the world, Paul became largely a man in isolation. When he died, there were only a few friends around him.

Paul Cain was like no other prophet I have met. His level of gifting and accuracy was unchallenged. I wrote a blog post about Paul on the day he died. Some thought I was too complimentary, while some thought I was unfair for ending the blog with these words: "He went to heaven under a dark, dark cloud."

Those who believe gifting is more important than character continue to sing Paul's praises. I am grateful for the good times I had with him. I learned so much about the prophetic from Paul. But I believe integrity matters—and even more so for the gifted.

This is the ugly side of the prophetic, gifted people caught in immorality, people who claim to speak for God when they clearly do not, and people who refuse to apologize when they are publicly exposed!

There are truths and verses in the Bible I don't understand. People who say things I would call blasphemy continue to thrive! I don't get it. However, I feel King Saul is a precedent that helps explain what I am talking about.

Although Ravi Zacharias was not part of the prophetic movement, he operated in a comparable way. He was gifted, and he exercised his gifting among thousands. When he died in 2020, he went out with people from all around the world singing his praises. Not since Billy Graham's funeral has a Christian leader received more praise and accolades at his memorial service. And yet, months later the news of Ravi's immorality became known. It seemed to me that God decided to use this to give the world a foretaste of what the final judgment would be like. God allowed Ravi's ugliness to be exposed, possibly as a warning to you and me of what God said to Moses, that "your sin will find you out" (Num. 32:23).

If you have unconfessed sin in your life, let these words drive you to your knees. When you hear of another's failure, fall, or getting found out, notice that prophetic gifting does not set apart the famous from the ordinary. You and I are what we are by the sheer grace of God.

As the great Southern Baptist preacher R. G. Lee's immortal sermon shows, people will reap what they sow: "Pay day, some day." Or, to quote Yogi Berra, "It ain't over till it's over." The reckoning will happen when God "will bring to light the things now hidden in darkness and will disclose the purposes of the heart" (1 Cor. 4:5).

This book is a fringe benefit in serving as a wake-up call to all of us.

Chapter 3

THE WORD AND SPIRIT

Our gospel came to you not only in word, but also in power and in the Holy Spirit.

— 1 THESSALONIANS 1:5

All Word and no Spirit we dry up. All Spirit and no Word we blow up. Both Word and Spirit we grow up.

— DAVID WATSON (1933–1984)

The well-known nineteenth-century minister Charles Spurgeon mentored many preachers. A young preacher once asked, "Mr. Spurgeon, could you help me? I am a fairly good preacher, but I don't see conversions."

Spurgeon replied, "Do you expect to see people converted every time you preach?"

The preacher answered, "Oh no, sir."

"That's the reason," responded Mr. Spurgeon.

The simultaneous combination of the Word and the Spirit

bring about expectancy. Expectancy is eagerness to see God at work in the salvation of people.

I believe another great awakening is coming. The next one will be like the Second Great Awakening of the nineteenth century. It will come suddenly. This coming awakening will include visual miracles and solid gospel preaching. As my friend Lyndon Bowring would say, those who come to hear will see and those who come to see will hear.

Problem of Imbalance

I see a problem in churches I visit and preach in all over the world—imbalance. Churches are either committed to gospel preaching or desperately seeking visible manifestations of the Spirit. When I speak about Word churches, I mean the type of churches that emphasize preaching and getting doctrine right. Churches that pursue healings, miracles, and other physical experiences I call Spirit churches. To find churches nowadays that are equally Word and Spirit churches is very rare.

Let me explain more about the emphases of Word and Spirit churches.

Word people stress the need for solid theology. They see their role as contending "for the faith that was once for all delivered to the saints" (Jude 3). Expository preaching and a rediscovery of justification by faith, assurance of salvation, and the sovereignty of God as taught by men like Martin Luther, John Calvin, and Jonathan Edwards are marks of Word churches. I agree that honoring God's name in these ways are essential parts of sound Bible teaching.

Spirit churches believe the honor of God's name will not be restored until we get back to the book of Acts, where the manifestation of signs, wonders, miracles, and the gifts of the Spirit was a normal part of following Jesus. Spirit churches expect places where prayer meetings occur to physically shake (Acts 4:31). They model their ministry after Peter's, whose shadow produced healing. On a truthful yet sobering note, Spirit churches also think it is possible for people to die if they lie to the Holy Spirit. We need that kind of power today.

Is it easier for a Word church to embrace the Spirit? Or for Spirit churches to embrace the Word? From what I have seen, Word churches sincerely believe they are already a Word and Spirit church. Likewise, Spirit churches that sincerely invite me believe they are already both. I am not their judge. But to find a church that adheres to solid theology, has consistent biblical preaching, sees regular conversions, and reports true miracles is rare.

The stark differences between Word and Spirit churches reminds me of another story about Charles Spurgeon. Because of the way Spurgeon viewed the importance of prayer and preaching, he was criticized by polar opposite theological traditions. He annoyed people that were unwavering in their own theological understanding by a prayer he uttered, "Lord, save thine elect and then elect some more."

One young and confused minister came up to Spurgeon asking, "But what if we save one of the nonelect?"

Spurgeon patted him on the shoulder and said, "God will forgive you for that." Spurgeon was called an Arminian by the Calvinists of his day, but the Arminians called him a Calvinist.

The religious leaders of Jesus's day had their own divisions.

Sadducees denied the resurrection and the spiritual world. Pharisees, on the other hand, believed in the resurrection of the dead. However, both groups considered themselves faithful to the Mosaic Law and tried to trap Jesus. When the Sadducees tried to uphold their teaching and trick Jesus with a story they had made up, Jesus said to them, "You are wrong, because you know neither the Scriptures nor the power of God" (Matt. 22:29). Jesus insulted Sadducees, who fancied they were experts on Holy Scripture. He was certainly bold to tell the Sadducees that they did not know their Bibles! Jesus also did the same thing with Pharisees. When Jesus taught the disciples on the Sermon on the Mount, he showed them that the Pharisees did not truly know the Mosaic Law (e.g., Matt. 5:17–20).

The way Jesus exposed his enemies was comical. In Matthew 22:29–33, Jesus exposed the Sadducees' ignorance by adding insult to injury when he explained the meaning of Exodus 3:6. To imply that the Sadducees did not understand Exodus 3:6 would be similar to saying that Christians today do not understand John 3:16. In Exodus 3:6, God said to Moses, "I am the God of your father, the God of Abraham, the God of Isaac, and the God of Jacob." Jesus used this well-known verse to show how faulty the Sadducees were by their denial of the resurrection of the dead. Jesus interpreted Exodus 3:6 as "He is not God of the dead, but of the living," which turned the Sadducees' doctrine on its head; this verse actually shows that Abraham, Isaac, and Jacob were *alive and well!* They were still alive and well by the power of God!

The Sadducees were not the slightest bit interested in the power of God. But Jesus showed that if they were to take the Scriptures seriously, they would see God's power in them! He made the Sadducees face an issue that had never gripped them.

I fear there are Word churches who are not the slightest bit interested in the power of God. They believe in the Scriptures, yes, but what about the power of God? They believe that power for individual believers to exercise the gifts of the Spirit from 1 Corinthians 12:8–10 was valid two thousand years ago, but not today. They are called "cessationists." They believe that the miraculous gifts ceased with the closing of the canon of Scripture. It is the Word only. Granted, they believe that a person is only converted by the work of the Holy Spirit. But they only view the Spirit soteriologically; namely, that the Holy Spirit *applies* the Word. The work of the Spirit to these believers is unconscious. But cessationists are only half right.

The Word and the Spirit

When I refer to the Word and the Spirit, I include all that cessationists believe about the Word being applied by the Spirit. However, there is more. There is the *immediate and direct* witness of the Spirit. The immediate and direct witness of the Spirit means the Holy Spirit can be *felt. Experienced. Consciously.* As Dr. Lloyd-Jones put it, how could the Galatians know they had received the Spirit (Gal. 3:2) unless it was something they consciously experienced?

By Word and Spirit I also mean the miraculous is alive and well, in that the gifts of the Holy Spirit (1 Cor. 12:8–10) are available today. Otherwise, what can new Christians think when they read 1 Corinthians 12:31, which commands us to earnestly "desire" (ESV) or "covet" (KJV) the best gifts?

When the Apostle Paul said that the gospel he preached

came "not only in word, but also in power" (1 Thess. 1:5), he implied that preaching the gospel *could* be done without power. For example, Dr. Lloyd-Jones used to refer to some Reformed people (Word people, generally speaking) as "perfectly orthodox, perfectly useless." I am embarrassed to say that most of my preaching over the years was largely in Word only.

I still personally dream of preaching with a level of power that I have not heretofore experienced.

I can indeed testify to once preaching with the level of anointing I always wanted. It happened during my series through Philippians, in chapter one, verse twelve. To my surprise and amazement, a high level of conscious anointing accompanied me when I preached. After I finished and took my seat next to the pulpit, I sat in awe and amazement. Everything was quiet. People did not get up or move around. I felt stunned and thrilled.

However, a major disappointment fell upon me no sooner than two hours later. One of our deacons, Graham Paddon, came up to me and said, "I have to tell you something you will not want to hear. The man who handles the sound system was sick this morning and forgot to call in. Your sermon was not recorded." My heart sank.

Another deacon came up and reassured me, "No problem. Aren't you scheduled to preach in Bromley this coming Thursday? Just repeat the same sermon." Good, I thought. However, when I preached that same sermon a few days later in Bromley, it was not the same. My notes were the same, but it was not even ten percent of the power God let me have *that one time*.

Why? You tell me.

The Holy Spirit is sovereign. We cannot twist his arm. We

cannot make him heal people. I cannot cause the anointing I long for to emerge, even if I went on a forty-day fast. Nor can you.

"Nobody said it would be easy" is the title of my friend Rob Parsons's latest book. Neither is it easy to bring the Word and Spirit at a high level. If it were, believe me, I would grab it with both hands.

That said, I believe that the simultaneous combination of the Word and Spirit, assuming the Spirit comes at a high level and the Word preached is solid truth, will produce spontaneous combustion.

What does this have to do with prophetic ministry or charismatics?

Ishmael or Isaac

In October 1992, Paul Cain and I had what we called a Word and Spirit conference at Wembley Conference Centre in London.

A few days before the conference I asked a charismatic leader, "If you were asked whether the charismatic movement was Ishmael or Isaac, what would you say?"

The leader answered, "Isaac."

Then I asked, "What if I told you the charismatic movement was, in fact, Ishmael?"

"Please don't say that!" he exclaimed.

I then realized how charismatics were going to react to the message I planned to give at the Word and Spirit conference.

I had two words to give at the conference. First, I shared my view that there has been a silent divorce in the church between the Word and the Spirit. When there is a divorce the children sometimes stay with the mother, but in other instances they stay with the father. In this divorce, you have those on the Word side and those on the Spirit side. Why did I call it a silent divorce? I cannot say when this divorce happened. That is why I called it a *silent* divorce. Perhaps the division was unconscious at first. I only know we have this situation—a divorce between Word churches and Spirit churches.

I knew my second word would not be well received. I told my audience that the greatest move of the Spirit we might imagine has not come yet. Most of them were charismatics, and they were not thrilled to hear what I said. This charismatic movement assumed that it was *the* great revival just before the second coming of Christ.

Remember, only a few days before this conference my conversation with the charismatic leader had prepared me for this reaction. The message I delivered went like this.

Abraham, an old man likely in his late seventies or early eighties with no heirs, was told by God to go outside his tent and count the stars. His wife, Sarah, was also old, and she was barren. There were so many stars in the night's sky that he could not count them. Yet God said to him, "So shall your offspring be" (Gen. 15:5).

Would Abraham believe such a word, he and Sarah being so old? It would have been understandable that Abraham's reply was something like, "You must be joking! How do you expect me to believe that?"

But Abraham did believe the promise. He believed God. And God counted Abraham's faith as righteousness (v. 6). The Apostle Paul used that Old Testament event as his Exhibit A for the doctrine of justification by faith alone.

We all know the promise to Abraham was not fulfilled right away. The years rolled on and not even one baby was born to Abraham and Sarah. Sarah suggested to Abraham a not-so-good idea: that he should sleep with Hagar, Sarah's handmaiden. That was not how Abraham had envisaged the way God's promise would be fulfilled, but he went along with that idea. They wanted to make God's promise come to pass themselves. But in doing so, they ran *way* ahead of the Lord.

Hagar became pregnant, then Sarah got angry with her. Hagar ran away in distress, but God stepped in and told Hagar to return to Sarah and to name her child Ishmael (Gen. 16:11). Since the child was male, Abraham concluded that Ishmael was the promised son, and he sincerely believed this for thirteen years. What else was he to believe?

But one day God stepped in and told Abraham that Ishmael was *not* the promised son after all. If Abraham had received this news that *Sarah* would conceive the promised child thirteen years sooner, he would have been thrilled. But not now. Abraham was not pleased. He pleaded with God, "Oh that Ishmael might live before you!" (Gen. 17:18).

Here was my word to the 2,500 people at the Word and Spirit conference in Wembley: Pentecostals and charismatics have believed *they* were God's ultimate promised movement to precede the second coming of Jesus. They were like Abraham while he believed Ishmael was God's promised son. Despite the ecclesiastical and ecclesiological differences between Pentecostals and charismatics, people generally believe that they have a lot in common. Although Pentecostals trace their beginnings to the Azusa Street Revival in 1906 and the charismatic movement to around 1960, they may be seen as one giant movement of the Spirit. In a word, they saw themselves as *the* promise of "Last Day Ministries."

However, I told them they were actually Ishmael. The many charismatic leaders present were deeply insulted. "You called us Ishmael?!" they exclaimed. In truth, I did.

I then stressed that Isaac would come. This was the good news: Sarah would have a son, and that son would be called Isaac (vv. 15–19). Just as the promise concerning Isaac was a hundred times greater than the promise regarding Ishmael, so will the next great move of God be a hundred times greater than the Pentecostal-charismatic movement. Although my audience cheered when I said that this movement will result in millions of Muslims being converted, the news that they were Ishmael was too much for some of them to bear.

A couple days after the Wembley conference ended, someone I did not know approached me and asked, "Did you get that idea from Smith Wigglesworth?" Early in the twentieth century, Pentecostals were wondering whether they were part of the mighty move of God the church had been expecting. When the prominent evangelist Smith Wigglesworth was asked about this, he said, "No." Wigglesworth then predicted a future movement that would be greater than both the Welsh and Wesleyan Revivals. It would cross over from Britain into Europe and spread all around the world. Three months before Wigglesworth died in 1947, he prophesied that a movement was arriving which would emphasize the baptism of the Spirit and the gifts of the Spirit. I did not know that he had prophesied something so similar. This was news to me—good news, comforting news. This meant that I was not the first to say something greater would come.

My personal conviction is that the best is yet to come. And I choose to call that best Isaac.

My Concerns about the Charismatic Movement Today

Three things concern me about present-day charismatics. First, the common denominator of Pentecostals and charismatics fifty years ago was the gifts of the Holy Spirit. Today, the focus is on prosperity teaching, which is sometimes also called "Name it and claim it" or "Health and Wealth." This teaching emphasizes that you should demand financial blessings from God. Second, the charismatic movement appears to believe its proponents can speak things or will things into being. Modern-day charismatics are trying to *make things happen*—including making Donald Trump president. Where is the trust in God's knowledge of the future or in God's sovereignty? Third, I mentioned earlier that dozens, if not hundreds, of sincere charismatic Christians prophesied that Trump would serve a second consecutive term in the White House. Why was his reelection so important to them? *Not a single one of them* predicted that Joe Biden would be inaugurated on January 20, 2021. Where are the apologies for getting this wrong?

It seems to me Ishmael has been exposed.

Like the way Jesus interpreted Exodus 3:6 for the Sadducees, I expect that the next move of the Holy Spirit will result in greater understanding of the most familiar verses in the Bible as well as undoubted signs and wonders.

One problem is that our minds are made up. We think we

know what this or that verse means. The commentaries have nuances, but generally agree on familiar passages such as John 3:16. However, I predict that when the next awakening comes, the Bible will not only be revered once again as infallible but will be like a brand-new book. People will read and devour it like they did in Martin Luther's day, when he turned the world upside down by his rediscovery of justification by faith alone. In a word, we will discover truth in God's Word that has been long hidden by our blindness and prejudices. As Jesus gave us his interpretation of the Law, the Psalms, and the Prophets (Luke 24:27, 44), so will the Holy Spirit shed light on passages we have hardly begun to explore, including the four Gospels and the rest of the New Testament.

When we read that "Jesus Christ is the same yesterday and today and forever" (Heb. 13:8), I equally believe that the Holy Spirit is the same yesterday and today and forever. And for that reason, we must strive for our churches and prophetic ministries to be Word and Spirit churches and ministries.

Chapter 4

THE GOD OF GLORY

When Joshua was by Jericho, he lifted up his eyes and looked, and behold, a man was standing before him with his drawn sword in his hand. And Joshua went to him and said to him, "Are you for us, or for our adversaries?" And he said, "No; but I am the commander of the army of the LORD. Now I have come." And Joshua fell on his face to the earth and worshiped and said to him, "What does my lord say to his servant?" And the commander of the LORD's army said to Joshua, "Take off your sandals from your feet, for the place where you are standing is holy." And Joshua did so.

—JOSHUA 5:13–15

I am a Christian not because of what it does for me, but because it is true.

—JONI EARECKSON TADA

Can you remember a time when someone you looked up to disappointed you?

My whole life has been shaped by preaching and preachers. What I liked about preachers, as well as prophets later in my life, was that they gave me a sense of God's presence. My lofty view of preachers eventually brought me disappointment. Sixty-five years ago, my favorite minister, a person I stood in awe of, was preaching in Chattanooga, Tennessee. I was a student pastor in the nearby city of Palmer. I journeyed there to have an hour with him and asked him to lay hands on me and pray for me. He did—I felt so honored. But as soon as he ended the prayer, these words followed: "Don't tell anyone my age."

I was so disappointed. He had let me down. I realized that my hero had only been thinking of his age the whole time his hand was resting on my shoulder. I did ask him how old he was—why was that such a big deal? Now all I remember about my prayer time with this person I looked up to was the end: "In Jesus's name, amen. Don't tell anyone my age." He was sixty-seven years old.

Since then, every person I began to admire a little too much eventually disappointed me sooner or later. This shows that the best of men are men at best, and it is an axiom we must keep in mind throughout this book.

I said earlier that this book is partly about prophets and partly about God. Prophetic people may fail to give God glory. They may get it right a bunch of times, but when they let you down it hurts. God, on the other hand, will not disappoint. God doesn't make mistakes. Scripture even tells us that it is impossible for God to lie (Heb. 6:18). That truth should give us confidence, just like it did for the early church.

Stephen, one of the original seven deacons, who became the first martyr of the church, has long been one of my heroes. What gripped me most was his anointing. I define "anointing" as being the power of the Holy Spirit that enables one's gift to function with ease. He had the gift of wisdom (Acts 6:3). Although Stephen was falsely accused by prominent Jewish leaders, his opponents "could not withstand the wisdom and the Spirit with which he was speaking" (v. 10). His gift flowed with ease.

Jesus promised that when people are called before the authorities to testify and defend the gospel, they should not worry in advance over what to say, "for the Holy Spirit will teach you in that very hour what you ought to say" (Luke 12:11–12). As we will see later, not all prophesying is of the same caliber. For example, a high level of prophetic power is promised to the one who is forced to defend the truth. The Spirit gave Stephen the words to say, and virtually all of Acts 7 are the words of Stephen before the Sanhedrin. I note that the very first word that Stephen utters before the Sanhedrin refers to God, whom he calls "the God of glory" (Acts 7:2). This tells me that the Holy Spirit wants you and me to regard the God of the Bible as the God of glory.

I wonder how many of us would have spontaneously thought to describe God that way? If not, why not?

When I went to Southern Baptist Theological Seminary in Louisville, Kentucky, in 1971, I was shocked to discover how many students and faculty resented that God wanted praise and glory. Some thought that needing praise and honor would make God weak. They did not like the idea of a jealous God. For example, Oprah Winfrey, whom I greatly admire, sadly turned away from her evangelical background when her pastor said that God was a jealous God.

One of the first things to be grasped about God is that he is the way he is because that is the way he always was and will be. He did not become a certain way over time. The way he *is* is the way he always has been and always will be—a God of glory. He did not create himself like this; the uncreated God always was, is, and is to come as a God of glory who wants worship and will not allow us to prefer another god before him. He wants praise and honor, and he is up-front about this. Jealousy is not a good quality in people, but God unashamedly says that even his name is Jealous (Exod. 34:14). The first two of the Ten Commandments reveal that God is "a jealous God" (Exod. 20:3–6).

This means God has a mind, an opinion, and will of his own. It cannot be changed. He does not need or want input or advice. He does not need a second opinion on what he decides to do. His mind is made up, one could say. Don't try to change him; it won't work.

So much theology in pulpits today, speaking generally, is not theology but anthropology. It is man-centered. People today ask, What's in it for me? Nobody seems to think to ask, "What's in it for God?" We are all a part of a "What's in it for me?" society. We live in the day of "entitlement." People demand their human rights, what (they believe) is "coming" to them. Jesus told us to seek first the kingdom of God and his righteousness, that other "things" such as food, shelter, and clothing will be added to us. The things that are added is a part of the package if we seek God first (Matt. 6:33).

The Bible is a God-centered book. It was written by people who were God-centered in their understanding of his ways. Our theology should be God-centered, a way of thinking that focuses on a God of glory. That was Stephen's God. And, in the words he preached, he showed us how Scripture reveals the God of glory.

But preaching about the God of glory got Stephen into a lot of trouble—even with Jews who should have known better. These Jews could not withstand the wisdom and Spirit with which Stephen spoke, and they killed him. Therefore, do not expect that great wisdom and power will overcome or change the minds of the adversaries of the gospel. Vindication is not guaranteed in this life but only in the age to come (2 Thess. 1:7–8).

Will you love God *as he is?* The answer you give to this question will have a huge bearing on your understanding of prophecy and prophetic integrity.

David Fellingham, an English hymn writer, grasped this. He wrote a great song that begins: *"God of glory, we exalt Your name, You who reign in majesty."*

The rest of that hymn is largely Holy Scripture, based on Ephesians 1. Many hymns written over two hundred years ago by men such as Isaac Watts, Charles Wesley, and John Newton had this in common: they were God-centered. The early Methodists learned their theology from the hymns they sang. When I consider many of the hymns written today, with few exceptions, I can see why our generation is so shallow in its knowledge of the Bible and theology.

The psalmist put it like this:

> The LORD is high above all nations,
>> and his glory above the heavens! (Ps. 113:4)

> Not to us, O LORD, not to us, but to your name
>> give glory,

for the sake of your steadfast love and your
faithfulness! (Ps. 115:1)

The angels cry to each other,

"Holy, holy, holy is the LORD of hosts;
the whole earth is full of his glory!" (Isa. 6:3)

God said through Isaiah the prophet:

"My glory I will not give to another." (Isa. 48:11)

One of the things we learn from Jonathan Edwards (1703–1758), a great revivalist preacher and theologian from early American history, is that neither the flesh nor the devil can produce in us a love for the honor and glory of God. If you love a God of glory, only *God* could bring this about in you.

Why is this important? Let me put this in terms of salvation to help you understand how loving a God of glory is the result of a supernatural work of God. I know of three ways of coming to a true assurance of salvation: (1) Looking directly to Christ and his death on the cross and not to our good works; (2) the immediate and direct witness of the Holy Spirit; and (3) knowing that you love the God of glory and honor. The flesh or the devil could not bring these about; only God himself can.

I owe a debt of gratitude to Dr. N. Burnett Magruder for impressing the teaching of the principles of the glory of God into my life and ministry. Dr. Magruder preached at my November 1964 ordination into gospel ministry at the Thirteenth Street Baptist Church in Ashland, Kentucky. He was a graduate of Yale University, where Jonathan Edwards had attended, and asked me some difficult and surprising questions about God's glory before a congregation of three hundred people. Dr. Magruder could tell that I was shaken to my fingertips, since it was (and still is) a fearful thing to enter gospel ministry. Later, I asked him, "Would you not agree that the highest devotion to God would be to die as a martyr for Jesus Christ?" He smiled, pulled out a pen, and wrote this on a sheet of paper, "My willingness to forsake any claim upon God is the only evidence that I have seen the Divine glory." I carried that piece of paper with me for many years, chewing on its implications. That was the most profound statement I have ever read in my life. Whether you agree or disagree with this statement, it mirrors a God that is unknown to most Christians today.

In the light of God's glory, we have no claim on God. The truth is, God's claim is on us. We are bought with a price (1 Cor. 6:20). He owes us nothing. And yet the polar opposite kind of thinking is widespread today, especially in the charismatic movement. Fifty years ago, all that charismatics would talk and preach about were the gifts of the Holy Spirit. Today, however, prosperity teaching is all too common. "Name it and claim it" is the current message of charismatics. Oddly enough, the focus for charismatics and many prophets is not on God's glory, but on the immediate needs and comforts of individuals.

I wish I did not need to say this: None of us has the right to snap our fingers and expect God to jump. Rather, we must approach God with the view of asking for mercy, no matter how long we have been Christians (Heb. 4:16).

Joshua

Joshua, Moses's successor, learned this sobering truth. He witnessed the unexpected and scary manifestation of God's glory shortly after leading the children of Israel into Canaan. A man with a drawn sword appeared to Joshua, and Joshua asked, "Are you for us, or for our adversaries?" (Josh. 5:13). It was a reasonable question. The answer, however, was "No" (v. 14). This was strange. It would make sense if the commander of the Lord's armies was on Joshua's side, on the side of the children of Israel. But no.

Joshua was to learn one of the most difficult, most profound, and most offensive aspects of the nature of the true God, namely, that God is a God of glory. He exists for his own glory. He wants praise. Worship. Honor. Adulation. He is unashamedly a jealous God. His name is Jealous (Exod. 34:14). He is on nobody's "side"; he sides with himself, with his own sovereign will.

I have noticed over the years that this is the very thing—that God is a God of glory and is on nobody's "side"—that often puts people off about the God of the Bible. They find this offensive. Horrible. What Joshua would discover about God is the polar opposite to teaching that plays into people's feeling of entitlement.

The first time I noticed how people were offended by a God of glory was when I was in seminary. I was truly surprised. The very God whom I had come to love and worship was the God many of the seminary students and faculty hated.

The Bible often speaks of the fear of God. But the "God" that many prefer would not harm a flea. And yet the "eternal gospel" is this: "Fear God and give him glory" (Rev. 14:7). The first message of the New Testament is that of John the Baptist: "Who warned you to flee from the wrath to come?" (Matt. 3:7). We are justified by Christ's blood and saved "from the wrath of God" (Rom. 5:9). Indeed, said Paul, Jesus "delivers us from the wrath to come" (1 Thess. 1:10).

Can you imagine the shock, the horror, the surprise, and the grief that people all over the earth will experience when they see Jesus in the clouds? Nobody seems to expect this. And yet "every eye will see him" and all men and women "will wail on account of him" (Rev. 1:7). Wailing. Let that sink in for a moment. How often do you ever hear a person *wail*? You may occasionally hear a sob or someone whimpering. But people only wail when there is no hope—none at all.

When I learned that the German philosopher Ludwig Feuerbach taught that God was nothing more than man's projection on the backdrop of the universe, I began to ask: whoever would have projected a God of glory? This shows how wrong Feuerbach was. People project the god they are comfortable with—one who is likeable. *No person would dream of loving a jealous God, a God who exists for his own glory.* This is the reason why Jonathan Edwards taught that the devil cannot produce love for the glory of God. If you love the God of glory and love the will of God—whatever it is—you may be sure that a work of grace has been done in you. The flesh can never create this. Feuerbach's God would never come up with this.

But if you discover that this is who God is and what he is like and then *love and adore* him, it means you are a genuine born-again child of God.

The chief reason that the Jews missed their own Messiah was because their respect for the God of glory had diminished to the point that their preponderant motivation was mutual acceptance of one another. They did not believe that Jesus was the Messiah, and Jesus told them why: *"How can you believe, when you receive glory from one another and do not seek the glory that comes from the only God?"* (John 5:44, emphasis mine).

Some sixty-five years ago, I sought to make John 5:44 the governing verse in my life. I partly received this conviction from a sermon I heard at Trevecca Nazarene College: that Enoch before his translation to heaven had this testimony, that he "pleased God" (Heb. 11:5). It does not say he pleased his friends. Or his enemies. Or his parents. Rather, he pleased God. I was thus given a burning wish to please God, since John 5:44 cohered so well with Hebrews 11:5. I certainly won't say I have reached this level of devotion; it is a very high standard. But it has given me peace when making my most difficult decisions and when my best friends and relatives did not understand the direction I chose. The approval that God gives provides infinitely more satisfaction than the praise and acceptance of people.

A God of glory was the God that Joshua encountered. He was on holy ground. Thus, he took off his sandals and worshiped just like his predecessor Moses had done years before (Exod. 3:5).

Moses

The "holy ground" experience of Moses and Joshua teaches at least two things. First, there are some things God does not want us to figure out. And, second, we must worship God despite not being able to figure out what we so eagerly want to figure out. I sometimes wonder if heresy is created by men worshiping logic more than truth and coming up with conclusions that are far removed from what God wants us to see.

God doesn't want us to know everything! God wants us to realize that we can only know for sure what *he* has chosen to make clear to us. God knows what is best for us to know. We cannot twist his arm. If we need to know something, God will reveal that to us when we need it. For example, Jesus told his disciples that he had many things to reveal but they could not bear them, at least not then (John 16:12). The problem is, many of us are like the disciples, who had no objectivity about themselves. Like them, we often fancy that we are ready for any level of truth or obedience. When Jesus asked the disciples if they were able to be baptized with his baptism, they hastily responded, "We are able" (Mark 10:39). In truth, they were *not* able; in Jesus's darkest hour they all forsook him and fled (Matt. 26:56).

In Exodus 3 Moses saw the burning bush that was not consumed and thought he would get close enough to that bush to find out why it didn't burn up. Who wouldn't like to know? Moses was only a few yards away when God said, "STOP. Don't come any closer. Take off your shoes. You are on holy ground." You and I cannot get one bit closer to God than God allows. The children of Israel, for example, were commanded to stay a thousand yards away from the ark of the covenant—a symbol of God's glory—as they approached the promised land (Josh. 3:4).

This should help us see that we can get only as close to God as he deigns. We cannot figure out or get to the bottom of certain truths that God does not want us to figure out or get to the bottom of. The burning bush incident should serve to caution us from implying that we have a close relationship with God so we can impress people. The worst kind of name-dropping is to use God's name in order to enhance people's esteem of you—like claiming "God told me"—whether it refers to our doctrine or experience. We will return to this later.

But let me give some examples of things we try to figure out. What do you suppose is the difference between what God predestines and what he allows? STOP. Don't try to figure that out because God will not allow you to figure that out. Why did God create humankind knowing that we would suffer? STOP. Don't try to figure that out. What is the difference between God knowing the future without causing it? STOP. Don't try to figure that out.

> For my thoughts are not your thoughts,
>> neither are your ways my ways, declares
>> the LORD.
> For as the heavens are higher than the earth,
>> so are my ways higher than your ways
>> and my thoughts than your thoughts.
>> (Isa. 55:8–9)

You and I should pray daily, "Help me, Father, to see what *you* want me to see, to believe what *you* want me to believe, to grasp what *you* want me to understand, and to be content with what *you* have chosen and not chosen for me to know." We may feel like we have the right motives to know more about God, but if we are not careful we will find ourselves trying to control God. He won't have this! We could be like Moses who wanted to get closer to God than God would allow. The truth is, if we could get as close to God as we wish, chances are we would not keep quiet about it. Thus, in a subtle way, we would seek to draw attention to ourselves. That does not please God. Part of the tendency of the human heart is to take ourselves too seriously. Jeremiah described you and me, "The heart is deceitful above all things, and desperately sick; who can understand it?" (Jer. 17:9).

I used to ask the members of Westminster Chapel: "How many of you could have tea with Her Majesty the Queen and keep quiet about it?" I will now ask you, the reader: Could you spend a night in the Lincoln Bedroom of the White House and never tell a soul? Could I? I doubt it.

What about a close relationship with God? We are promised that if we draw near to God he will draw near to us (Jas. 4:8). A close relationship with God would be evidenced by our willingness to forsake any "claim" upon him. That means we need to love the will of God—to dignify his will—whether or not he makes us feel good by answering all our prayer requests.

Jesus knew what was "in man" (John 2:25) and therefore knows how much to reveal to us. This is because he is a God of glory. He will never, never, never share his glory with another (Isa. 42:8).

May I ask whether you have difficulty with a God like this?

I understand. He is more mysterious than we will ever grasp while we are on this planet. He is greater than anything that can be said about him. Does this thrill you? If not, I am not saying you are not a Christian. But I am saying you most certainly *are* a Christian if you *do* love and worship a God like this.

Holy ground. I cannot think of anything more awesome than being on holy ground.

I believe that true prophets of God—that is, those who

take off their shoes whether or not they receive assurance that God is on their side—would wait on God before being too quick to speak.

Another way of putting it is this: are you a servant of God merely because of what God does for you, or do you serve God because his Word is true?

Chapter 5

THE GLORY OF GOD AND THE DIGNITY OF HIS WILL

*Moses said, "Please show me your glory." And [God]
said, "I will make all my goodness pass before you and
will proclaim before you my name 'The LORD.' And I will
be gracious to whom I will be gracious, and will show
mercy on whom I will show mercy."*

—EXODUS 33:18–19

*But [Stephen], full of the Holy Spirit, gazed into heaven
and saw the glory of God.*

—ACTS 7:55

*What is the glory of God? It is who God is. It is the
essence of his nature; the weight of his importance;
the radiance of his splendor; the demonstration of his
power; the atmosphere of his presence.*

—RICK WARREN

In 1975, I was pastor of the Calvary Baptist Church in Lower Heyford, Oxfordshire, England. Owing largely to the influence of my previously mentioned mentor, Dr. N. B. Magruder, I wrote a catechism for both young and old people. Since I had been thrilled, challenged, sobered, and mystified by God's glory, I based the catechism upon some principles of the glory of God. Apart from Dr. N. B. Magruder's influence, I hate to think of what the shape of my theology may have become.

One question and answer from my old catechism was:

Question: What is the greatest thing a person can do?
Answer: To see and love the glory of God.

God graciously raises up people we all need at strategic times in our lives to guide our thinking. The members of my church in Oxfordshire were largely U.S. Air Force men with only a high school education. It was thrilling to see how they leaped at the opportunity to learn theological principles I sought to teach through this catechism. Thankfully, many testified that it changed their lives.

My primary understanding of the glory of God is that it is *the dignity of his will*. There are various notions about the glory of God. My perception comes from Ephesians 1:12, where we learn that we have been predestined by God to obtain an inheritance "to the praise of his glory." I would point to God's sovereign will as in Moses's original request, "Please show me your glory" (Exod. 33:18). In response, God said, "I will be gracious to whom I will be gracious, and will show mercy on whom I will show mercy" (v. 19). Paul quotes the latter verse in Romans 9:15, a section that describes God's will in action with examples from Israel's history. In other words, I see this understanding of God's glory as paramount.

To see God's glory as the dignity of his will leads the way to all other concepts of his glory. For example, God's glory is manifested by displaying the supernatural, creating signs and wonders. Consider his *visible* glory of the pillar of cloud and the pillar of fire in the desert (Exod. 40:38). The glory of God may be manifested in *hearing* God's voice, as Moses experienced when he received the Ten Commandments (Exod. 19–20) or when the disciples heard God speak on the Mount of Transfiguration (Mark 9:7; 2 Pet. 1:17). There is also God's *invisible* glory, namely, what is *felt*, as in the fear of God or a high level of joy. For example, when Jesus raised a man from the dead, "fear seized them all" (Luke 7:16). When tongues of fire appeared on the heads of the one hundred and twenty on the Day of Pentecost, it was a manifestation of God's glory (Acts 2:1–4). When God struck Ananias and Sapphira dead in front of people watching, "great fear came upon the whole church" (Acts 5:11). And yet people were not scared away, but "more than ever believers were added" (v. 14).

More invisible examples of the supernatural manifestations of God's glory include the *fruit of the Spirit* (Gal. 5:22), the unity of the Spirit, and the people of God loving one another. These may seem ordinary, but they are examples of a beautiful and invisible manifestation of God's glory. There are times when God manifests his presence in a way that words cannot describe:

> All those who find thee find a bliss
> Nor tongue nor pen can show;

> The love of Jesus, what it is,
>
> None but his loved ones know.
>
> —BERNARD OF CLAIRVAUX (1090–1153)

At Westminster Chapel many of us entered a prayer covenant in which we prayed daily for the manifestation of God's glory along with "an ever-increasing openness in us to the way God *chooses* to manifest that glory." God's glory manifested itself through our street—in witnessing, prayer ministry, and praying for sick people by anointing them with oil. We hoped this prayer covenant would result in great revival. But I believe God did manifest his glory in us after all by moving us into humble ministry.

It was a manifestation of the glory of God when Philip was given a holy nudge to go to the desert and approach a man in a chariot (Acts 8:26, 29). When God spoke to Paul prophetically, "I have many in this city who are my people" (Acts 18:10), referring to men and women who were not even converted yet, that also was a manifestation of the God of glory.

I would commit a big oversight if I neglected *natural* manifestations of God's glory. "The heavens declare the glory of God, and the sky above proclaims his handiwork" (Ps. 19:1). Paul speaks of this at the beginning of Romans, "For what can be known about God is plain to them, because God has shown it to them. For his invisible attributes, namely, his eternal power and divine nature, have been clearly perceived, ever since the creation of the world, in the things that have been made. So they are without excuse" (Rom. 1:19–20).

If we are totally honest with ourselves, we would prefer to see or feel more of the supernatural manifestations of God's glory, since they can build up one's faith. We may, therefore, likely experience God by witnessing and sensing what has *no natural explanation.*

A service in Ashland, Kentucky, on April 13, 1956 changed my life in an unexpected way. Something like smoke, a fog, or a haze settled on the congregation for several minutes. People saw it but did not know what to make of it. Looking back on that experience, I believe there was a seal of God on the service. Pastor Jack Hayford also has described a similar moment. He looked into the empty auditorium of his church in California one Saturday and noted that it was inexplicably filled with a haze. "It's what you think it is," Jack felt the Lord speak to him. From that experience of the manifestation of God's glory, his church grew and grew from three hundred to several thousand.

When I wrote the catechism influenced by Dr. N. B. Magruder, I was being blessed by my study of the English Puritans at Oxford. Not only that, but I was also indebted to the friendship of Dr. J. I. Packer and Dr. Martyn Lloyd-Jones. That time was when I first defined the glory of God in my catechism as *the dignity of his will*, a definition my friends seemed thrilled with.

Can you see how my own definition of the glory of God leads to thinking about other aspects of his glory? No definition, however apt, can explain God; he is greater than anything that can be said. But it is my deep conviction that God's sovereign will is what all of us must come to affirm about his glory *before* we can honor him as we should. The absence of solid teaching and a consistent understanding of the sovereignty of God explains the superficiality of the church today. Understanding the dignity of God's will should lead us not only to worship him but to be careful about how we speak in his name.

The glory of God is the sum total of all his attributes—his omniscience (he knows everything), his omnipotence (he is all-powerful), and his omnipresence (he is everywhere). His glory says it all.

The will of God reflects who he is, what he wants, and what he chooses and purposes to do regarding his creation and his people. God always has and always will have a will of his own. He does not need input from you or me to decide what he needs to do next. This is so difficult to understand because time is not a limit for God; he is not waiting to act. The petition in the Lord's Prayer, "Your will be done, on earth as it is in heaven" (Matt. 6:10), makes us aware that the Father already *has* a will and wants us to obey and honor that will. In heaven there is no rebellion; the angels are perfect worshipers of God. God's will is what we must try to love and what we must submit to if we mean what we say when we pray the Lord's Prayer.

A Sense of Sin

It is impossible to remain the same when you think about or experience the glory of God because you will get a sense of your sin. That is why I object to prophetic ministry that is not accompanied by gospel preaching.

Even the great prophet Isaiah reminds us of this fact. He had been in the ministry for years, but one day it was given him to see a vision of the glory of the Lord. The seraphim cried one to another, "Holy, holy, holy is the LORD of hosts; the whole earth is full of his glory!" The result: Isaiah exclaimed, "Woe is me! For I am lost; for I am a man of unclean lips . . . for my eyes have seen the King, the LORD of hosts!" (Isa. 6:1–5). There was no doubt about Isaiah's credentials; he was the prophet. But when God's glory showed itself, he could only cry out, "Woe is me!"

While writing this very book, I was invited to be on a religious TV show to discuss one of my books, *Chances Are, You Might Be a Pharisee If* . . . I made the observation that the Pharisees did not have a sense of sin and that the present-day church also lacks this sense. I also said that if you read the biographies of men and women in church history, the greatest saints always saw themselves as the greatest sinners.

The TV interviewer was flummoxed; he looked uneasy. We still had another fifteen minutes to discuss the book, but I could tell that he wanted to cut the interview short. It was obvious that discussing a sense of sin with this man was utterly foreign to him. He had nothing to say. I tried to help, referring to the Lord's Prayer, "forgive us our trespasses," and quoting 1 John 1:8, where John said, "If we say we have no sin, we deceive ourselves, and the truth is not in us." He forced a smile and concluded, "Thank you for being with us today, Dr. Kendall," ending the program.

What really matters?

I invited cross-carrying Arthur Blessitt to preach for me six consecutive Sunday evenings at Westminster Chapel in 1982. He called one of his sermons "The Heartbeat of God." It was about soul winning, the need to see lost people saved. This was an epochal moment in my ministry, if not also for Westminster Chapel. I needed that sermon as much as anyone, because it flowed out of a vision; Blessitt had seen the glory of the Lord as he was carrying the cross alongside the Amazon in South America. The content he preached, inspired by that vision, cohered with my teaching about the glory of God. That sermon showed me how I could bring more honor to God by dignifying the *reason* God sent his Son to die on a cross, namely, that people would believe. But how can they believe unless they hear the Word they need to be saved (Rom. 10:13ff)?

What matters most to God? His glory and honor. The glory of God is the common denominator of God and his ways throughout the Old Testament. This same common denominator also runs throughout the New Testament. This God of glory is unveiled in the book of Revelation, when the four living creatures and the twenty-four elders fall down and worship him:

> "Worthy are you, our Lord and God,
> to receive glory and honor and power,
> for you created all things,
> and **by your will** they existed and were
> created." (Rev. 4:11, emphasis mine)

What matters most to God is the *glory of his Son*, the eternal *Logos* made flesh, the one who died on the cross for the sins of the world. The same living creatures and elders worship the Lamb:

> "Worthy are you to take the scroll
> and to open its seals,
> for you were slain, and by your blood you
> ransomed people for God

> from every tribe and language and people
>   and nation,
>   and you have made them a kingdom and priests
>   to our God,
>   and they shall reign on the earth."
>   (Rev. 5:9–10)

That said, do you suppose it matters to God when we focus on politics more than the reason Jesus died on the cross? Are we more interested in who is president than seeing people coming to the Lord Jesus Christ in faith? Is our focus on preserving our comfortable way of living rather than promoting the honor and glory of God?

Arthur Blessitt was right. He said the heartbeat of God is seeing the lost saved. God gets the ultimate glory when we affirm what his Son did by dying on a cross. After all, this is why God "sent" his Son (John 3:17). This is *why* Jesus died on the cross. The eternal *logos* was made flesh in the person of Jesus of Nazareth, who was (and is) the God-man. He was man *as though* he were not God; he was God *as though* he were not man. Jesus *was and is* one hundred percent God and one hundred percent man. As he was writing many years later, John reflected on his days with Jesus: "We have seen his glory, glory as of the only Son from the Father, full of grace and truth" (John 1:14). The glory of God was manifested in his eternal Son who died on a cross to save the world.

We should think about this in a time when we are drawn to trust in political solutions, when political solutions may not be what truly matters to God after all.

How does understanding the nature of God relate to

prophecy? Would not a true prophet have foreseen that Joe Biden would be the next president? If you are a true prophet of God, why did God not tell you this? Do you believe God is omniscient and knows the future?

Chapter 6

DOES GOD KNOW
THE FUTURE?

*"Therefore, thus says the LORD, Behold, I am bringing
disaster upon them that they cannot escape. Though
they cry to me, I will not listen to them."*

—JEREMIAH 11:11

*"I am the Alpha and the Omega, the first and the last,
the beginning and the end."*

—REVELATION 22:13

A God who does not know the future is not God.

—ST. AUGUSTINE (354–430)

*Every experience God gives us, every person he puts in
our lives, is the perfect preparation for a future only he
can see.*

—CORRIE TEN BOOM (1892–1983)

Do you believe the inauguration of Joe Biden took God by surprise?

When prophets speak disinformation, they portray a different image of God than the God of the Bible. Many prophetic people are misrepresenting God, and their mistaken words are giving the impression that God is unreliable. The present theological crisis is not a challenge to the existence of God, but rather about his nature. However, the Bible does unveil a Creator God whose existence and nature are inherently trustworthy and reliable. God began his work by saying, "Let there be light," and instantly "there was light" (Gen. 1:3). He made humankind in his own image; he created us male and female (v. 27). He made us with a free will before the Fall (Gen. 2). He promised Adam and Eve he would punish them if they disobeyed him (Gen. 3). They sinned, and then God punished them by allowing death to come upon all humankind (Rom. 6:23). Did the sin of Adam and Eve take God by surprise? No: the lamb that was slain on the cross was foreknown from the "foundation of the world" (1 Pet. 1:20).

When people in a prophetic role rise up and say they have a word from the Lord, in the eyes of others they represent God. When those words of knowledge or predictions are wrong, people have a choice to make about the prophet, the message, or God. Many questions arise: Was God unaware? Does God care about what is going on in the United States? Could this person speaking to you be wrong? Can I trust this person? Can I trust God?

We face a severe crisis—perhaps even two. We have a crisis of leadership within the charismatic movement that predicts one thing while another happens. How long will we let this continue? However, the greater crisis is theological because

God cannot be both all-knowing and mistaken about who will be president.

Does God know the future?

You may already believe that God knows the future. But I am going to show (and remind) you of a few Bible verses that make the answer to the question crystal clear.

> "I am God, and there is none like me,
> declaring the end from the beginning
> and from ancient times things not yet done,
> saying, 'My counsel shall stand,
> and I will accomplish all my purpose.'"
> (Isa. 46:9–10)

> "But concerning that day and hour no one knows, not even the angels of heaven, nor the Son, but the Father only." (Matt. 24:36)

The Old Testament prophet Isaiah unquestionably depicts God as like no other. God's knowledge of the future is certain (unlike our limited foresight), because the creation has already happened. And in the book of Matthew we learn that God's knowing of the exact date and hour of the second coming of Jesus is all the proof we need that he knows the future.

Old Testament Prophecy and Future Events

But I will say more from the Old Testament about God's knowledge of the future, which he communicated to the prophets.

Joseph, the favorite son of Jacob, predicted that his eleven brothers and his parents would one day bow down to him (Gen. 37:5–9). This was perfectly fulfilled over twenty years later (Gen. 45:1ff). Joseph also predicted to Pharaoh that there would be seven years of plenty followed by seven years of famine. All happened exactly as Joseph prophesied (Gen. 41:25–57).

Jacob called his twelve sons and said, "Gather yourselves together, that I may tell you *what shall happen to you in days to come*" (Gen. 49:1, emphasis mine). The patriarchal blessing was prophetic and set the stage for Judah and his offspring to be the bloodline of the Messiah (Gen. 49:8–12; Matt. 1:2–3; Luke 3:33).

Jeremiah was accused of treason for prophesying that Israel would be taken to Babylon for seventy years, showing that God knows the future:

> "This whole land shall become a ruin and a waste, and these nations shall serve the king of Babylon seventy years. Then after seventy years are completed, I will punish the king of Babylon and that nation." (Jer. 25:11–12)

Hananiah, a false prophet, told everyone what they wanted to hear, claiming that the captivity would end after two years (Jer. 28:1–3). But Jeremiah stepped in and said to Hananiah, "The LORD has not sent you, and you have made this people trust in a lie. Therefore thus says the LORD: 'Behold, I will remove you from the face of the earth. This year you shall die.'" That very same year, "in the seventh month, the prophet Hananiah died" (vv. 15–17).

Indeed, all prophecy in the Old Testament and the New Testament, right through the last book in the canon of Scripture, assumes that God knows the future. St. Augustine affirmed this by saying that a God who does not know the future is not God.

A Pivotal Time in My Life: 1955–56

On October 31, 1955, I had what I like to call a "Damascus Road experience." It occurred just after 6:30 a.m., when the glory of the Lord filled the car as I was driving from Palmer to Nashville on old U.S. Route 41 in Tennessee. I love taking friends to the spot where it happened. During this experience, I sensed two verses coming to me: 1 Peter 5:7 ("casting all your anxieties on him, because he cares for you") and Matthew 11:30 ("my yoke is easy, and my burden is light"). At the time this vision occurred, my spiritual burden was heavy and getting heavier. I wondered what was going on. Was I not saved? Suddenly, as I was driving along, I saw Jesus interceding for me at the right hand of God. It was so literal. It was more real to me than anything I had ever known—more real than the Tennessee countryside around me. I burst into tears and stopped praying. I was a spectator and simply watched as God took over. I was overwhelmed with Jesus showing such love for me, although I could not make out what he was praying. The next thing I remember was an hour later while I was driving through the town of Smyrna. I heard Jesus say to the Father, "He wants it." The Father answered, "He can have it." In that moment I felt a warmth go into my chest, just like in John Wesley's "strangely warmed" experience when he felt the assurance of his salvation. The peace and joy exceeded all I had ever experienced. I did not know one could have peace like that. It was not merely the cessation of anxiety; it was the presence of indescribable peace.

The next thing I can recollect was pulling into the parking lot near Tidwell Hall, my Trevecca dormitory. I went to my room and shaved, then went to my 8:00 a.m. class and wondered about what had just happened to me.

That experience in the car left me with a sense of God's presence the whole day and changed my theological perspective. The afterglow lasted nearly a year. I had visions. In one vision I saw that great revival would go around the world. I saw people all over the globe shaken with the knowledge that Jesus really is the Son of God and is coming in judgment. That vision is obviously unfulfilled; I still hope that I will see it in my lifetime.

I also had visions concerning other people. One day Ralph Lee, my roommate at Trevecca, was jilted by his girlfriend. As I listened to Ralph pouring out his grief, I had an open vision of his future wife as clearly as if I was looking at her photo. I assured Ralph that the girl who jilted him was not the one he would marry, but that he would marry a pretty redheaded lady (who was not a student at Trevecca). Four years later Ralph brought his lovely wife and first child to our home in Florida. She was the exact young woman I had seen in my vision.

In February 1956 I began serving in a student pastorate at a church in Palmer. Unexpectedly, I was persuaded to resign on Sunday, May 6, setting May 20 as my final Sunday. Although those dates initially seemed clear to me, it crossed my mind later that I should take a look at the calendar to make sure both were Sundays (they were). In early June 1956 as I was driving home to Ashland, Kentucky, I noticed that my dashboard looked exactly like the one in Ralph Lee's 1953 Chevrolet. That was strange. Why would my dashboard look exactly like Ralph's? I eventually discovered that it was to prepare me for something rather traumatic which happened a couple months later. My father and grandmother, who had bought me a new 1955 Chevrolet to travel from Trevecca to my student pastorate in Palmer, were not pleased with my change of theology and direction that would lead me away from my Nazarene church background. My dad even said that I would have to pay rent if I chose to stay at home—and I had no job. As I shared this with some friends, a man named Marvin Creamans overheard the conversation. "I'll give you a job," he responded. As soon as I got into his car to pick up and deliver clothes for Creamans Quality Cleaners in Ashland, I noticed that it had the 1953 Chevrolet dashboard which I had seen in my vision. This gave me comfort and a sweet assurance that God was truly leading me.

Before you get the wrong impression, not all of my visions were fulfilled as I expected. Some remain unfulfilled; perhaps I misinterpreted them or maybe they were symbolic. I did not seek out these visions. I did not think it was not up to me to figure them out or even to make them happen.

My father was very upset with me in those days. He was the godliest man I knew, so he meant well when he accused me of breaking with God. I shared one of my visions with him to help him see that I had not betrayed God, and also revealed my conviction that I would have an international ministry.

Dad had one question for me: "When?"

"One year from now," I hastily and unwisely replied.

He asked me to put that in writing! And I did.

However, twelve months later I was not in the ministry at

all but was working as a salesman. Dad thus felt fully vindicated in his perception of my theology and relationship with God. I was still a mere door-to-door salesman, selling vacuum cleaners and strollers. I doubt whether any human being on the planet would have held out hope for my vision about the future.

The last vision I will share was especially unusual, and I had to wait a few years to discover the outcome.

While still in Tennessee during 1956, I had a very odd vision of my father wearing a mint-green summer suit and walking down the center aisle of a modestly sized church. I had no idea where it was, although I remember that there were windows on the right, but none on the left. The auditorium contained less than two hundred theatre-like seats without cushions. I had a sinking feeling that my future was tied to such a place as that. Fast forward to January 1960, when I agreed to preach in a small church in Ohio. I immediately noticed the center aisle and the theatre-like seats with windows on the right, but none on the left.

In July 1960 I became the minister of that small church, the Carlisle, Ohio, Church of God congregation (headquarters in Anderson, Indiana). A month later my dad phoned to say that he and Abbie (my stepmother) would be driving to Carlisle to hear me preach on Sunday. Immediately I said to Louise, "Dad will be wearing a mint-green summer suit." When they arrived on Saturday, my father handed me a mint-green summer suit to hang in the closet for him to wear the next day. During the service I kept waiting for the vision to be fulfilled, determining not to make anything happen. It was not until the service ended that my dad made his way out of the church, but then turned back and walked down the center aisle. It happened just as I saw in the vision.

What was the purpose of that vision? I can only conclude that it was the gracious provision of God to comfort me and to give me assurance that I was in his will. I only stayed at that church for eighteen months, but this vision (alongside others) gave me hope for a better future than I had anticipated up until then. Although I continued to be a salesman for some years after, I felt more optimistic about my future ministerial prospects.

I would not build my theology of the omniscience of God from this vision or any of the others I had. Furthermore, I am not a prophet; I am a Bible teacher. I base my theology (I believe) entirely on Holy Scripture. But I will admit that my own supernatural experiences cohere with the premise that God knows the future. And he knows it perfectly.

I remember hearing George Beverly Shea say one day before he sang at a Billy Graham meeting: "Don't worry about the future. God has already been there."

Doesn't God Need Me?

I don't mean to be unfair, but some people love a God who neither knows the future nor knows what he will do tomorrow without their help. Those people perplex me. Are they afraid of an all-powerful and all-knowing God? Do they really trust themselves to have a hand in the future? Do they have more confidence in themselves than in a sovereign God?

How does God answer prayer if he does not know the future? I ask that question because one of my seminary professors embraced open theism and candidly admitted that he does not believe God answers prayer except when people ask him for help. According to him and others that embrace open theism, he also does not believe that God will listen to my prayer and make things happen apart from my help or initiative. Moreover, God *needs* my help; otherwise, nothing will happen.

You may ask, why should I pray to a God who already knows the future? The same God who knows what we need even before we ask him (Matt. 6:8) commands us to pray! If you ask, "Why witness to the lost if God already knows who will be saved?" my answer is that God told us to preach the gospel to every person (Matt. 28:19; Mark 16:15). It is a matter of obedience to believe what God teaches about his knowledge of the future. It is equally an exercise in obedience to honor him by praying and witnessing to the lost.

God is in control. Indeed, Jesus sat down at the right hand of God the Father and controls the universe from there (Heb. 1:3). All things are subject to him. You may object, "At present, we do not yet see everything in subjection to him" (Heb. 2:8). Yes, this is true, but it is also part of God's plan. The writer of Hebrews agrees: "But we see him who for a little while was made lower than the angels, namely Jesus, crowned with glory and honor because of the suffering of death, so that by the grace of God he might taste death for everyone" (v. 9).

Why believe when disaster like the COVID-19 pandemic strikes? We see Jesus. Why believe when God allows evil? We see Jesus. Why believe when all hell seems to break out before us? We see Jesus.

The word *antinomy* is relevant here. Antinomy refers to parallel truths that appear to be irreconcilable but which are actually both true. For example, God could have chosen to save the world apart from preaching. But in his wisdom he chose the "folly" of what is preached (1 Cor. 1:21). God could work without his people praying, but Jesus still taught us to pray and not give up (Luke 18:1). Indeed, God uses those who don't give up, even when the future seems hopeless.

Yogi Berra had answers for most questions. If he were a pastor he would probably say, "It ain't over till it's over." I had the privilege of meeting Yogi Berra a few years ago, when he kindly agreed to endorse my book, *It Ain't Over Till It's Over*, and asked him, "When did you first say, 'It ain't over till it's over'?" Yogi told me a story about when he was the manager of the New York Mets (later the San Francisco Giants). His team was at the bottom of the National League standings, and people were calling for his resignation. The future looked bleak. A reporter asked him in July, "Is it over, Yogi?" He replied, "It ain't over till it's over." As it turned out, in September the Mets finished first, winning the National League pennant! If one does not give up at the natural level, how much more should we as believers take seriously Jesus's word to pray and never give up!

Sometimes people will not persist. For example, a Baptist pastor in Kentucky was angry with God because his daughter had died at an early age despite the church's fervent prayers for her healing. He publicly announced that "God has a lot to answer for," turning away from the Bible and embracing open theism in his bitterness.

I can sympathize with those who say God has a lot to answer for. I do not understand *why* he created and sustains a world which has such a prevalence of evil, agony, sorrow, suffering, wicked judges, crooked politicians, war, earthquakes, tornados, and injustice. However, the difference between the Kentucky pastor and me is that I learned to side with Habakkuk.

Habakkuk

The Old Testament prophet Habakkuk had four complaints against God that remind me about present-day complaints (Hab. 1:2–17):

1. Why didn't God answer Habakkuk's prayer?
2. Why did God allow suffering?
3. Why did God allow injustice?
4. Why did God side with the enemy of Israel?

Even though each question or complaint may have nuanced answers, the complaints can be summarized under question number two: Why does God allow suffering?

In response, God made a kind of deal with Habakkuk. Habakkuk decided to go to a watchtower and wait for the revelation (Hab. 2:1) that would explain *why God allows suffering*. The Lord answered Habakkuk only to tell him that the revelation, or vision, awaits for its appointed time. Habakkuk had thought the answer would be at hand. Yet when he got to the watchtower, God showed up only to give a prophetic word that the revelation awaits an appointed time in the *future*: "it hastens to the end" (v. 3). End? What end? You could call it the end of the world. You might call it the last day. We today could call it the second coming. God implied that Habakkuk would have to make a choice: *whether to believe the promise or walk away*.

God added that the revelation would be delayed—that it will tarry. It may seem slow in coming, but we need to wait for it. Thousands of years have now passed, but we need not worry because God said in so many words to the anxious prophet that the vision will definitely come. It is worth waiting for.

By the way, you and I are still waiting for it.

Habakkuk had a choice to make when God put this proposition to him. He needed to either accept God's promise or shake his fist at God. In other words, Habakkuk could have said to God, "You must be joking. You are just kicking the can down the road, delaying the answer and making me wait a long time."

Thankfully, Habakkuk chose to believe God's words.

And in these words, God included a very significant promise: the righteous shall live by faith (v. 4). This verse gets quoted three times in the New Testament; Paul uses it twice in his teaching on justification by faith alone (Rom. 1:17; Gal. 3:11). The verse also appears in the book of Hebrews to strengthen discouraged Christians who needed to wait for God to show up (Heb. 10:38).

Rather than getting bitter and questioning God for the rest of his days, Habakkuk rejoiced because he believed *that God knew the future* and that God would clear his name. We are not told what mental processes Habakkuk went through. We only know that something happened to Habakkuk. Remember also that Habakkuk lived in an agrarian society; it needed sun, rain, and good weather to exist. Rather than holding on to his anger, Habakkuk affirmed:

> Though the fig tree should not blossom,
>> nor fruit be on the vines,
> the produce of the olive fail
>> and the fields yield no food,
> the flock be cut off from the fold
>> and there be no herd in the stalls,

> yet I will rejoice in the LORD;
> I will take joy in the God of my salvation.
> GOD, the Lord, is my strength;
> he makes my feet like the deer's;
> he makes me tread on my high places.
> (Hab. 3:17–19)

Can you and I say that? Are you like so many who praise God only when they are thriving in their comfort zone? Or do you praise God only when your prayers get answered quickly? I urge all who read these lines to be like the prophet Habakkuk, believing and rejoicing in God's promise.

Abraham

In Scripture, one of the first major figures to base his faith in the fact that God knows the future is Abraham. Dear reader, I ask you to bear with me as I repeat a bit of what I said earlier. I think that Genesis 15 is essential to both the theme of this chapter and our doctrine of salvation.

One evening Abraham was very discouraged. He was a wealthy man, but had no one to leave his wealth to since he had no children. He was advanced in years, and Sarah, his barren wife, was some ten years younger but past the age of bearing children. He thought to himself, "Am I to leave my wealth to my servant Eliezer?" At that moment God instructed Abraham to go outside his tent and look up at the stars. "Number them," God said. It was a clear night, but the stars were too many to count. There were dozens. Hundreds. Thousands. We now know there were billions! God said to childless Abraham, "So shall your off-spring be" (Gen. 15:5).

Abraham had a choice to make. He could choose to believe God's promised prophecy. Or he could have said something like this, "You must be joking. Are you are teasing me? Do you really expect me to believe that Sarah and I will have a son at our age? Don't be unfair like that."

If Abraham had those thoughts or spoke those words, we never saw them in Scripture because "He believed the LORD, and he counted it to him as righteousness" (v. 6).

As we saw earlier, this account in Genesis became the Apostle Paul's exhibit A for his teaching on justification by faith alone. In Habakkuk we saw a prophet deciding to "live by his faith," trusting that God knew the future. Likewise, Abraham was counted righteous for believing that God knew *the future.*

Yes, God knows the future. It is one of the truths that qualifies him to be God. A sovereign God. An omniscient God.

Paul said, "Therefore God has highly exalted [Jesus] and bestowed on him the name that is above every name, so that at the name of Jesus every knee should bow, in heaven and on earth and under the earth, and every tongue confess that Jesus Christ is Lord, to the glory of God the Father" (Phil. 2:9–11). Whereas these verses merely say that every knee *should* bow, Paul elsewhere refers to the future, for "we *will* all stand before the judgment seat of God" (Rom. 14:10, emphasis mine). He then quotes God swearing an oath:

> "As I live, says the Lord, every knee shall bow
> to me,

and every tongue shall confess to God."
(Rom. 14:11)

God knows the future perfectly. Time is on his side. He will clear his name, and we who have cleared his name in advance will rejoice on that day when all see that the God of the Bible actually is just as he is described in it—true and just.

In the meantime, God shares his secrets with those who fear him (Ps. 25:14 KJV). "For the Lord GOD does nothing without revealing his secret to his servants the prophets" (Amos 3:7).

The true prophets of God foresee things because God knows the future.

Chapter 7

SEVEN LEVELS
OF PROPHECY

Do not despise prophesies, but test everything; hold fast what is good.

—1 THESSALONIANS 5:20–21

Every word of God proves true;
  he is a shield to those who take refuge
    in him.
Do not add to his words,
  lest he rebuke you and you be found a liar.

—PROVERBS 30:5–6

I don't make mistakes. I just make prophecies which immediately turn out to be wrong.

—MURRAY WALKER OBE, SPORTSCASTER

Charismatics get excited when the preacher reads from chapters 12 through 14 of 1 Corinthians. They know they will hear "earnestly desire the higher gifts" and "earnestly desire the spiritual gifts, especially that you may prophesy" (1 Cor. 12:31; 14:1). Paul lists nine gifts of the Spirit in 1 Corinthians 12, and I see a hierarchy of importance assigned to the gifts. Also, in 1 Corinthians 14 Paul tells the church that prophecy is greater than tongues because "the one who prophesies builds up the church" (v. 4). Since the gifts of the Spirit are different in terms of importance and relevance, I will show you that there are seven levels of prophetic gifting.

Before I get to the levels, I want you to notice something about the nine gifts of the Spirit: wisdom, knowledge, faith, healing, miracles, prophecy, distinguishing between spirits, kinds of tongues, and interpretation of tongues (1 Cor. 12:8–10). Four of these gifts are revelatory. Revelatory means that the Holy Spirit makes a person aware of something. With the gift of wisdom the person knows exactly what to say. Knowledge helps a person know what is true. The discerning of spirits helps people in the church recognize the Holy Spirit vis-à-vis the counterfeit or demonic. And, lastly, prophecy is a unique bit of information about the present or future. The difference between a word of knowledge and a prophetic word is subtle. A word (utterance or message) of knowledge could refer to theological truth or it may reveal a person's need. It may also refer to the present or past; on the other hand, prophecy largely refers to the present or future.

In addition to urging us to seek the higher spiritual gifts, Paul elsewhere says that the gifts and calling of God "are irrevocable"—or, as the KJV says, "without repentance" (Rom. 11:29). This is another example of an antinomy in Scripture: Surely, seeking a high-level spiritual gift would cause the seeker to please God by a close walk with him by repentance. And yet any degree of repentance does not guarantee that one will receive a high-level spiritual gift, because at the end of the day all spiritual gifts are given sovereignly. That is why Paul says, "[the Spirit] apportions to each one individually as he wills" (1 Cor. 12:11).

The question is, when Paul urged the Corinthians to earnestly desire the spiritual gifts, "especially that you may prophesy" (1 Cor. 14:1), was he encouraging Christians to aspire to be the next Elijah? Was Paul suggesting that another Samuel or Habakkuk or Joel would emerge as one sought the gift of prophecy? Of course, it may have been possible that a Christian in Corinth had a secret wish to be a prophet like Elisha (2 Kings 2:15) or Deborah (Judg. 4:4). Was Paul challenging the Corinthians to be Samuels or Daniels? Was he laying a foundation for prophets in the church just as in ancient Israel?

Theologian Wayne Grudem thinks the answer to these questions is no. Dr. Grudem says in his book *The Gift of Prophecy* that the New Testament use of the word "prophecy" does not refer to a prophetic office, which did exist in Old Testament times. In the New Testament church there were people giving prophecies, which was a normal practice. However, the messenger or the prophet was not important; rather, the prophecy, the message, was paramount. After all, the gift of prophecy, not tongues, edifies the church.

Paul urged the Christians in Rome to be careful not to think of themselves more highly than they ought to think, but to think soberly according to the "measure" of faith that God had given or assigned (Rom. 12:3). The same Greek word, *metron*, is used in John 3:34 to show that Jesus had the Holy Spirit "without limit" (NIV) or "without measure" (ESV).

A few years ago, I read Romans 12:3 every day. I needed it, and it was a sobering experience. I learned that we all have a limit to our faith and to our gifting. I know by experience how humbling it is to admit what our limits are. But it is critically important that you see God as the source of any power you have and recognize and stay within the faith he gives you. When you try and move beyond the power God gives you, you are asking for trouble.

The other thing I learned from Romans 12:3 was that God never promotes us to the level of our incompetence. That means God can use me just as I am, no matter how inferior I might be when compared to other preachers.

One of the most difficult, if not most embarrassing things we ever have to do, then, is to come to terms with the limit of our faith, gifting, or anointing. Nobody can do everything. This is a challenge to our pride. Nobody has all the gifts described in Romans 12:6–8, which are sometimes called motivational gifts. Too many of us fall prey to what is sometimes called the "Peter Principle"—that every person is promoted until reaching a level at which he or she is no longer competent. Some of us want a higher profile in the body of Christ, so we sometimes impute to ourselves an ability or gift that God has not put there. Some pull strings to get the larger church or receive the most prestigious invitation. Ultimately, many who do this end up in burnout or worse, fulfilling the Peter Principle.

Would you want a gift that God does not want you to have?

That said, I suggest seven levels of prophetic gifting. Imagine a pyramid, starting with the lowest-level gifting at the bottom—a word of general exhortation—and ending at the top with Holy Scripture—the ultimate level.

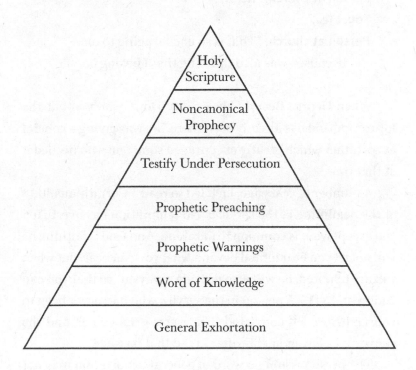

Holy Scripture

Noncanonical Prophecy

Testify Under Persecution

Prophetic Preaching

Prophetic Warnings

Word of Knowledge

General Exhortation

Level Seven: General Exhortation

The late Dr. Michael Eaton (1947–2017), whom Westminster Chapel supported, was a missionary to Nairobi, Kenya. He called the general exhortation "low level prophecy." A word of general exhortation can come from any Christian who wants to be a blessing to the body of Christ. You may do this exhorting publicly or privately. For example, you may walk across a church auditorium and say to someone,

> **You:** "How good to see you here today. I have a feeling
> you belong here."
> **Person at church:** "Really?"
> **You:** "Yes."
> **Person at church:** "That is so encouraging to me,
> because I was also thinking that I belong here."

When George Beverly Shea said, "Don't worry about the future, for God has already been there," he was giving a general exhortation which greatly encouraged someone who needed it at that time.

A number of years ago, I felt led to read 1 Corinthians 10:13 at the beginning of the service: "No temptation has overtaken you except what is common to mankind. And God is faithful; he will not let you be tempted beyond what you can bear. But when you are tempted, he will also provide a way out so that you can endure it" (NIV). A person in the service who had never been to church before felt convicted. That verse gripped her, and she converted a few moments after I read that passage!

The person issuing a word of general exhortation may not sense any special unction of the Spirit but only feels a desire to pass on a word that seems fitting. Someone can make a huge difference in another person's life just by saying something simple like this, "It is no accident that you are here; God has a purpose for you today." A word like that, should the Holy Spirit own it, can be life-changing. Even when the Holy Spirit applies the word, the person giving the exhortation may have no idea that it resonated with anyone.

A word of general exhortation might be given by the person leading worship. For example, I remember hearing a person start a service by saying, "Let's worship and sing in a way that gives God pleasure." That phrase gripped me. I never thought of giving God "pleasure" by my singing—this made me want to sing better!

Low level prophecy can bring pleasure and glory to the Most High God and stir the hearts of everyone. There are no qualifications for giving a general exhortation. You can do it. I can do it. Elijah could do it. The Apostle Paul could do it. We all can do it, blessing the body of Christ and giving praise to God.

Level Six: Word of Knowledge

An utterance, message, or "word of knowledge" may be sound teaching or a personal word about what is happening or has happened in a person's life. Based on my reading of the New Testament and pastoral experience, one does not need to have a high level of spiritual gifting like Old Testament prophets to receive a word of knowledge for someone. This is also the sort of thing Paul had in mind when he urged people to prophesy.

That said, those with a high-level prophetic gift can always operate at the level of general exhortation or word of knowledge. But those who operate at the level of prophesying that Paul has in mind in 1 Corinthians 14 should not fancy themselves as Elijahs or Nathans. God could grant this, of course. But people should be cautious not to think more highly of their gift than what God "assigns"; remind yourself often of Romans 12:3.

The teaching of Gary Morgan, a highly respected prophetic teacher from Australia, helped me understand that the umbrella of revelation encompasses three things:

1. The "word of knowledge" is revelation from heaven about a past or present situation. For example, Samuel revealed to Saul where his missing donkeys were (1 Sam. 9:20).
2. The "word of wisdom" is revelation that surpasses human knowledge or intellect, as in the case of King Solomon (1 Kings 3).
3. The "word of prophecy" is the foretelling of future events.

A word of knowledge can be spectacular, such as when someone reveals names, addresses, or phone numbers. It can also be more ordinary, like when a timely and edifying word is given.

An unspectacular example of a word of knowledge in my life happened to my wife, Louise. One Sunday, she went to Westminster Chapel with a heavy heart. Someone at the Chapel had previously been very rude to one of our children, so she was dreading going back to church. But as soon as Louise arrived, a Nigerian convert from Islam named Grace rushed to her and said: "Sister Kendall, I don't know what this means, but I have to share a word with you: *jealousy.*" Louise immediately burst into tears, because she indeed needed to hear that word at this very moment. Grace had no idea why this particular word had been given to her, but she felt like God wanted her to pass it on to Louise. Note that Grace did not say, "The Lord told me," but Louise was convinced that God *had* told Grace to say that!

The final part of that story is a crucial point in this book. To say "The Lord told me" does not make the Lord look good, because this statement focuses on the person who makes the claim. Saying "The Lord told me" misuses the name of the Lord; it is merely name-dropping. No matter how deeply people feel that they have a word from the Lord, they *do not need to make this claim.* Instead, they should let their hearers see for themselves that this word is from the Lord!

About ten years ago, a lady came up to me at a C.L.A.N (Christian Leaders Across the Nation) gathering in Scotland. She said, "I keep sensing that there is something concerning your *heart* whenever I see you." I asked her if her sense referred to my physical heart, which she confirmed. Consequently, when I got home I asked to have an echocardiogram, which revealed that I needed immediate open-heart surgery. I often wish I could see that lady again, for it was the only time I ever met her. That was a word from God for me that saved my life, but she did not say that the Lord had told her this.

Bethan Lloyd-Jones, wife of Martyn Lloyd-Jones, once told me a story about Evan Roberts, the leading figure in the Welsh Revival (1904–5). A young man with a broken heart had walked many miles to meet Evan Roberts. He found the house where Roberts was staying and knocked on the door. The young man urgently asked to have a word with Mr. Roberts, but did not explain his desperate request to the host of the house. The host then went upstairs to Roberts's room, saying that someone needed to talk with him. However, Evan Roberts was in prayer and would not come down to meet the young man. The host then began pleading with Roberts just to greet the man, who was now very distraught. Roberts still refused to go down, but did give the host a message to pass along to the young man: "Give him Psalm 27:10." This verse reads: "When my father and my mother forsake me, then the LORD will take me up" (KJV). The young man had indeed been rejected by his parents and turned out of his home, so this timely word ended up being more powerful and consoling than if he had personally met Evan Roberts. The young man left rejoicing that God knew his situation.

As you can see, a word of knowledge can be immensely encouraging to someone in a crisis. This "low level" prophecy is unspectacular, but it is pure gold to the person who needs it.

Level Five: Prophetic Warnings

Warnings come in different forms. Two personal stories about warnings follow, as well as a series of prophetic warnings during Paul's return to Jerusalem.

I received a warning in January 2020. I had just finished speaking at a church in Lafayette, Louisiana, and a man who knew we were scheduled to leave for Britain the following week said to me, "Don't worry if you don't spend your full six months in England this year. If you have to return home sooner, it is part of God's plan." That was a rather odd word, and I was unable to shake it off. We were only in London a short time before cases of COVID-19 spread through the city. On March 15 we flew back to the United States, and we felt consoled that God had kindly prepared us for this sudden change of plans.

Here is a much earlier example of a warning I received. In January 1951, when I was sixteen and living in Ashland, Kentucky, Dr. W. M. Tidwell—a noted holiness preacher—came to our church one Sunday. At the close of the service Dr. Tidwell, aged eighty, said, "Someone here is getting their last call to be saved." The atmosphere in the service immediately became quiet and sober. Dr. Tidwell then announced to the host pastor, "I am not going to close this service; you close it." However, the pastor refused to close the service, so people slowly got up from their seats and went home without receiving a formal benediction or closing prayer.

The next day I came home after finishing my newspaper delivery route. My mother came out crying, "Have you heard about Patsy?"

"What happened?" I replied.

"She was killed on her way home from school," my mother answered.

My mother then recalled that she had sat near Patsy Branham in church the previous day, feeling uncomfortable over Patsy mocking what was going on during the close of Dr. Tidwell's service.

I never got over that tragedy. Every time Louise and I visit Ashland, the memories of that Sunday come back to me. At 25th and Montgomery Avenue two cars had clashed and killed Patsy, whom I had known well. Was that a warning for the congregation? Was it a warning for Patsy? Was it a warning for me? The only thing I can say for sure is that this incident had cemented in me a keen sense of the fear and judgment of God.

When the Apostle Paul began heading for Jerusalem in Acts 20, people warned him not to go there. He told the elders in Ephesus that he was going to Jerusalem, "constrained by the Spirit"—his mind was made up. He admitted that the Holy Spirit had testified to him that "imprisonment and afflictions" awaited him. Nevertheless, added Paul, he did not regard his life as having any value, nor was it "precious" in his own sight (Acts 20:22–24).

When Paul arrived at Tyre, unnamed disciples who did not appear to be part of any rank or hierarchy were the first to warn him. According to Luke, "through the Spirit" they told Paul "not to go on to Jerusalem" (Acts 21:4). If one takes the view that Luke, who wrote both the gospel of Luke and Acts, was under the inspiration of the Holy Spirit, it would seem that God himself was warning Paul not to go to Jerusalem. Otherwise, Luke surely would not have said that the disciples warned Paul "through the Spirit."

The next day Paul and his party came to the house of Philip, who had four unmarried daughters exercising prophetic gifts. One can readily surmise that they too warned Paul (vv. 7–9).

More examples came along. Agabus, whom Luke called a prophet, "took Paul's belt and bound his own feet and hands and said, 'Thus says the Holy Spirit, "This is how the Jews at Jerusalem will bind the man who owns this belt and deliver him into the hands of the Gentiles"'" (v. 11). This same Agabus had previously prophesied "by the Spirit" about a great famine arising over all the world in the days of the Roman emperor Claudius (Acts 11:28).

How did Paul respond to these prophetic warnings? The same Paul who told the Thessalonians not to despise prophecies now says: "What are you doing, weeping and breaking my heart? For I am ready not only to be imprisoned but even to die in Jerusalem for the name of the Lord Jesus." When they realized he would not be persuaded, "we [this would have included Luke] ceased and said, 'Let the will of the Lord be done'" (Acts 21:13–14). There is little doubt that Luke himself was on the side of those who believed Paul should not go to Jerusalem.

Who was right? Were the prophets who warned Paul right? Was Paul right?

Paul felt constrained by the same Spirit who Luke says inspired these prophetic people. You can easily see both sides. Paul was indeed mistreated in Jerusalem and imprisoned. But was Luke right in siding with those who prophesied in the Spirit that Paul should not go there? As for Agabus, he broke the rule I am putting to the reader in this book by saying "Thus says the Holy Spirit" (v. 11). Did Agabus take himself too seriously? This is possible. A close look at the way everything turned out did *not* match everything Agabus said (see Acts 21:27–26:32)!

A good case can be made that both Paul and these prophets heard from God. God willed for Paul to go to Jerusalem and then go to Rome in chains.

And yet a case can be made that New Testament prophecy and Old Testament prophecy were not on the same level. Paul did say elsewhere, "Prove all things; hold fast that which is good" (1 Thess. 5:21 KJV). If a prophet's message was wrong during Old Testament times, this meant that the prophet had to be stoned. However, there is no such warning in the New Testament; we are instead encouraged to not close our minds to prophecies while still being careful to test them. When an Old Testament prophet said, "Thus says the Lord," such a word was not open to scrutiny. Wayne Grudem has argued that the successors to the Old Testament prophets were the apostles chosen of God. They were the ones with undoubted authority, not, for example, those Christians in Corinth whom Paul encourages to prophesy while allowing for their scrutiny: "Let two or three prophets speak, and let the others weigh what is said" (1 Cor. 14:29).

Level Four: Prophetic Preaching

The first motivational gift Paul refers to is prophecy: if one's gift is prophecy, it should be done "in proportion to our faith" (Rom. 12:6). The word translated "proportion" in Romans 12:6 is *analogia*, from which we get the word "analogy." Some interpret the word for prophecy in Romans 12:6 to mean preaching. It certainly includes preaching—but it is more than that. If one's exposition of Scripture is *truly* an unfolding of God's Word, it is prophetic. One does not have to refer to the future for a word to be prophetic. One may speak as "oracles of God" (1 Pet. 4:11) and therefore be prophetic. This means at least two things: (1) stay within your anointing, or gifting, since Paul elsewhere tells us not to "go beyond what is written" (1 Cor. 4:6). (2) It refers to sound theology—"analogy of faith." This means comparing Scripture with Scripture. Whether Romans 12:6 is carried out by a "prophetic word," as we are examining in this book, or by preaching, its caution is for us to be sound in doctrine. Good teaching and preaching coheres with the entirety of Holy Scripture.

In my own experience with prophetic people, I have seen that they generally lack solid theology. Some don't know their Bibles! When I explained the gospel to Paul Cain, I got the feeling he was hearing it for the first time. To his credit, he grabbed it quickly—Paul Cain was saved when I shared the gospel with him. But it was odd that someone so gifted had such a poor understanding of the gospel.

Don't get me wrong; I am not suggesting that the many people today who love to prophesy do not have a valid prophetic gift. However, my conviction is that people with prophetic gifting should be very careful about what they teach. As I mentioned earlier, the Apostle Peter said that such people should speak as if their words were the "very words of God" (1 Pet. 4:11 NIV; "oracles" in ESV and KJV). This is what all pastors, vicars, bishops, and preachers wish for.

Prophetic preaching can energize an entire sermon. For example, the sermon I preached at Wembley Conference Centre in October 1992 in which I likened the charismatic movement to Ishmael and forecasted that Isaac would come was prophetic preaching.

Prophetic preaching may also be a book. I regard two of my books as prophetic: *We've Never Been This Way Before* (Charisma House, 2020) and *Whatever Happened to the Gospel?* (Charisma House, 2018). In the former I state why I believe America is under judgment but that there is hope. In the latter I show why the gospel has generally passed behind a cloud but that the true gospel will restore life to the church.

Regarding books, critical feedback is a form of testing or weighing the message. There is no magic in our words, although some feel that way. One of my publishers once told me a story about an author that refused editing because "every word in my book is from God." This is utter nonsense—we all need editing, advice, feedback, encouragement, and criticism. The problem with most of us, as Somerset Maugham (1874–1965) put it, is that when we ask for criticism we really want praise.

Prophetic preaching might be short. A sentence or two inserted in the right place of a sermon might speak prophetically. Or perhaps prophetic preaching is accidental, comparable to a word of exhortation. Accordingly, preachers may be unaware that they said anything prophetic. For example, many preachers know what it is like to have a listener come up to them after the sermon and say, "How did you know I was here today? You spoke as though you knew everything about me."

A well-known Bible verse among prophetic preachers and teachers is most relevant here: "For the testimony of Jesus is the spirit of prophecy" (Rev. 19:10). This testimony should govern all prophecy. The book of Revelation is literally called "the revelation of Jesus Christ" (Rev. 1:1), and is thus prophecy. And, for that matter, so is every book in the Bible. Peter referred to the Old Testament as prophecy: "No prophecy of Scripture comes from someone's own interpretation. For no prophecy was ever produced by the will of man, but men spoke from God as they were carried along by the Holy Spirit" (2 Pet. 1:20–21). Paul also virtually said the same thing: "All Scripture is breathed out by God and profitable for teaching, for reproof, for correction, and for training in righteousness" (2 Tim. 3:16).

When the Apostle John wrote down the words, "The testimony of Jesus is the spirit of prophecy," he meant that all *true* prophecy comes from Jesus Christ himself. Prophecy will mirror the person and truth of Jesus. A clue to what this means is to remember that the letters to the seven churches in Revelation 2 and 3 are the very words of Jesus who sits at the right hand of God. Jesus spoke as a prophet in his days on earth, graciously including people like the woman of Samaria. He prophesied about changes in worship (John 4). But in his glory Jesus is seen as having eyes like a flame of fire, feet like burnished bronze, and a voice like the roar of many waters (Rev. 1:12–16). He knows everything going on in his church (Rev. 2). Many prefer to separate the Jesus of the Gospels from the Jesus who addresses the seven churches, as if they were different persons. Lest we forget, some of the prophecies Jesus issued during his earthly ministry were harsh, especially the seven woes to the scribes and Pharisees (Matt. 23). The testimony of Jesus will therefore reflect not only the love and tenderness of the Father but also his justice and anger.

I hope I'm not being unfair, but many prophets today only give words of encouragement with the aim of making people feel good. I'm sorry, but such prophecies do not mirror the full image of Jesus, especially as revealed in the book of Revelation. The testimony of Jesus, therefore, means that the prophecy is not only true but in accordance with the entire Word of God.

Level Three: Testify Under Persecution

The ability to speak with clarity under persecution requires a high level of prophetic authority and power. Jesus speaks about this reality: "When they arrest you, do not worry about what to say or how to say it. At that time you will be given what to say, for it will not be you speaking, but the Spirit of your Father speaking through you" (Matt. 10:19–20 NIV). This is the only promise I know of in Scripture that we can be sure we are speaking God's words, and it is given to those suffering persecution. For example, in Acts 6 and 7 Stephen was forced to answer his critics. We would expect him to be fearful, but he was not afraid to speak.

Jesus gave us two examples for how Matthew 10:19–20 applies to us: (1) We are under pressure from persecutors, and (2) we do not plan what to say but answer as needed. These words remind us that all who live godly in Christ Jesus will suffer persecution (2 Tim. 3:12). And we should not be surprised if we are suddenly required to give an answer for what we believe. Thankfully, Jesus did tell us, "Do not worry about what to say," so that we won't be afraid and trust in our own power. The only command here is not to worry—the Spirit will be with us in an indescribable way!

Obviously, this is a very high level of anointing of the Holy Spirit. You and I cannot go out looking for it, and we cannot work it up. Most Christians in the United States, including those with powerful prophetic gifts, will never experience this level of prophecy.

I experienced what may be likened to this level of power once, during my tenure as the pastor of the church in Carlisle, Ohio (the one where my dad once wore the mint-green suit; see chapter 6). I had accepted the call to this church because they insisted they "had no creed but Christ, no law but love, and no book but the Bible." That was initially good enough for me, but eventually things turned out differently. A group from the church accused me of preaching that Jesus was God and that God was able to secure the response of anyone he effectually calls to salvation. They reported me to the church authorities of that denomination, and by September 1963 they had set up a heresy trial for me. At that time, it was the severest tribulation of my life. Providentially, my morning reading for the day of the trial was Matthew 10:19–20, which assured me that God would give me the words to say. And it worked—I was calm during the trial proceedings. Every word flowed out smoothly. I wish I could have that level of power when I preach!

I also experienced one lesser but still memorable illustration of this power when I was in Jerusalem in July 2002. Canon Andrew White, the archbishop of Canterbury's envoy to the Middle East, phoned to say, "Yasser Arafat will see you in Ramallah tomorrow evening at 6:00 p.m." I phoned Louise, who was in the States, to ask her to pray for me. I was allowed to bring two friends with me, so I brought Lyndon Bowring and Alan Bell. I had no right to do it, since I was not being persecuted, but I decided to claim the words in Matthew 10:19–20 about taking no thought concerning what I should say as my weapon for meeting the famed Palestinian president. Lyndon and Alan quietly interceded for me, praying in the Spirit. During the meeting I was calm, not unlike what I had experienced in Ohio in 1963. A visit that should have lasted only fifteen minutes went on for almost two hours. I watched tears come to Arafat's eyes as we talked. Seeing it as an evangelistic opportunity, I stressed again and again that Jesus died on the cross for our sins (contrary to the Islamic belief that Jesus did not die on a cross). Arafat followed us out at dusk while the Muslim call to prayer was echoing all over Ramallah. He wanted me to come back to see him again. What an eerie feeling. I ended up visiting him five more times. While I refused to think about what to say on this first visit, I did not use the same approach on subsequent visits because I planned in advance what to say to Arafat. After all, I was not persecuted—although meeting with a world leader for the first time was an extraordinary circumstance. When Yasser Arafat died two years later, I wept.

St. Augustine offered an interesting observation regarding a high level of anointing under persecution. He reckoned that if God could grant this power and authority when we are called to testify under persecution, he could just as easily grant this kind of power when we preach. After all, as I noted a little while ago, Peter did say that when we speak we should speak as one speaks the "oracles" of God. If that special type of speech were ever granted to someone, he or she need not claim to be speaking that way! Rather, let others sense it.

Stephen's persecution resulted in his speaking the very words of God—Acts 7 is almost completely Old Testament Scripture from start to finish. And at the close of his message, the church's first martyr saw Jesus "standing" at the right hand of God (Acts 7:55). How could this be, since the Bible says Jesus is now "seated" at God's right hand. Bethan Lloyd-Jones gave the best answer: "Jesus stood to welcome the first martyr home."

Level Two: Noncanonical Prophecy

The Old Testament prophets who did not write Scripture are the ones I have in mind here. This is a very high level; in fact, this is the highest level any prophetic person can aspire to. It doesn't get higher, stronger, or more powerful than this. As we will see in a little while, only Scripture is higher, stronger, and more powerful. But nobody will ever prophesy with authority equal to Scripture. And if they say they do, disregard them. By noncanonical prophecy, I mean that the speaker has power and authority like Old Testament prophets such as Elijah, Elisha, Nathan, and Gad. These were men owned of God, whose prophetic words came directly from him. But they were not canonical prophets—that is, unlike Ezekiel, Jeremiah, Daniel, and Isaiah, they did not have books named after them.

The question is: can there be noncanonical prophets like Elisha and Elijah today?

My answer: maybe. It would be extremely rare. I am leaving the door open for this, for two reasons. First, Jesus Christ is the same yesterday and today and forever (Heb. 13:8). There is not a single verse in the Bible alerting the body of Christ that the era of so-called cessationism would be coming down the road—whether with the death of the oldest apostle (John) or the time of the formation of the canon of Holy Scripture. When was the canon decided, after all? Some say in the early part of the fourth century; some say the latter part of the fourth century; and some say the latter part of the seventh century. The teaching of cessationism—that the miraculous gifts exercised by individual believers ceased with the closing of the canon of Scripture—is utter speculation. Sadly, some have turned this theory into a dogma and made it normative. In my view, this categorically quenches the Holy Spirit.

Here is the irony. Generally speaking, I am on the side of the cessationists when it comes to sound theology. I read their writings, listen to their sermons, and hear their public interviews. My heart warms to what they teach. At the same time, however, my heart aches for them! I say to myself, "Why can't these people also be open to the immediate and direct witness of the Holy Spirit?" Some claim to be open, yes, but often this is only in their heads. Some do not call themselves cessationists, but they might as well be. I'm afraid some cessationists tend to find fault with nearly every move that purports to be the work of the Spirit. I advise a loving caution: be careful that you don't hastily dismiss a possible move of the Spirit because it seems new and different, especially if it is not occurring in your own church!

Let us remember that the Holy Spirit, like God the Father and God the Son, is the same yesterday and today and forever. For example, Jesus said that he himself did nothing but what he saw the Father do (John 5:19). The Holy Spirit, like Jesus, speaks not on his own authority but what he hears (John 16:13). A non-canonical prophet like Elisha and a canonical prophet like Joel or Micah had this in common: they said what they said by the power and direction of the Holy Spirit. The Holy Spirit did not begin to exist on the day of Pentecost! He is the eternal Spirit (Heb. 9:14) who existed in eternity before the world began, just like the Father and the Son. It was therefore the same Holy Spirit that is in all Christians today who led holy men of old, as 2 Peter 1:20–21 says. Furthermore, as Jesus was given the Spirit without any limit (John 3:34)—which is true of him *alone*—it might please God to raise up a Nathan or Deborah today to speak with a *large measure* of the Spirit. This would not be at the level of Scripture, but could possibly be equal to noncanonical prophets like Elisha or Nathan.

I put these thoughts to you, the reader, as a Bible teacher, not a prophet. I do so with fear and trembling.

We must never forget that God's ways are higher than our ways and he loves to confound the "sound" theologians of this world. If God could turn stones into children of Abraham in John the Baptist's day (Luke 3:8), he could raise up another John the Baptist if he so chose! In a word: We must never, never, never underestimate God's next move or limit him by being locked into a theological grid. We must never forget that God's ways are higher than our ways. Remember that Paul's proclamation of Christ crucified was a "demonstration of the Spirit and of power, so that your faith might not rest in the wisdom of men" (1 Cor. 2:4–5).

There are only one or two men whose prophecies were so extraordinary that they made me think of Elisha. I would not be surprised if more such individuals would show up in the future. Some present-day prophetic people claim to be in the Elisha category. Perhaps they are—but I doubt it. If they are, they are probably not among those who prophesied Donald Trump's second term in the 2020 election. I could be wrong, since God is a gracious God, and I would want to welcome those who have sincerely repented for getting their prophecies wrong. And I will tell you why I would give them a second chance: not merely because they got it wrong but because they seem to have the humility of a Nathan or Samuel.

Jeremiah Johnson is an example of a contemporary prophet with integrity. He predicted that Trump would win victory in 2020, along with many others. But Jeremiah Johnson was the first one (as far as I know) to reverse his position and admit that he got it wrong. I gather he received a heap of criticism for humbling himself.

As for those who will not admit to their error, I certainly hope they are not like King Saul. Strange as it may seem, the Spirit of God did come on Saul and he prophesied with such awesomeness that people around him asked, "Is Saul also among the prophets?" (1 Sam. 19:23–24). This event happened at the same time Saul was on his way to kill David. Figure that out! My only biblical basis for not giving up on failed prophets comes from Romans 11:29, which says that the gifts and calling of God are irrevocable. Some would say that this verse only refers to Israel, but my interpretation is that a general principle already existed, which Paul applied to Israel as an example.

After God rejected Saul and revealed the news to Samuel, Samuel went to the house of Jesse to anoint the next king. However, Samuel too hastily assumed Eliab was the next king (1 Sam. 16:6). Prophets are not devoid of personal prejudices, and it was natural for Samuel to suppose Eliab was the man because in ancient Israel the firstborn got double the inheritance. But God stepped in: "Do not look on his appearance or on the height of his stature, because I have rejected him. For the LORD sees not as man sees; man looks on the outward appearance, but the LORD looks on the heart" (v. 7). Samuel pretty much admitted right in front of Jesse and his sons that he was wrong in supposing that the next king would be Eliab. It turned out that young David, the last person anyone would have imagined, was anointed as the next king (vv. 12–13). Fortunately, Samuel preferred listening to God rather than pleasing Jesse.

We all have our personal biases—theological and political. It is so easy to impose our strong prejudices on Holy Scripture, thus infiltrating our teaching and preaching. For example, consider how Nathan the prophet had to admit he got his words wrong. Nathan initially told King David that he should build the temple, and this was exactly what David wanted to hear. But when Nathan got home, God said to him (in so many words): "I did not tell you to say that. You must go back to David and tell him that he *cannot* build the temple" (see 2 Sam. 7:4–17). Did Nathan dig in his heels and say, "God, my prophetic reputation is at stake. I cannot do such an embarrassing thing"? No. He humbly went back to David to tell him that one of his sons would build the temple (v. 12ff). Thankfully, David took the news with dignity (vv. 18–29).

If one should be trusted by God to prophesy at the same level as Elisha or Nathan, can one say "Thus says the Lord"? I answer: Why do it? I would say that if you are an Elijah and Elisha and Gad and Nathan rolled into one, follow Jesus's own interpretation of the third commandment in the Sermon on the Mount to refuse to invoke the name of the Lord. It is not necessary to bring anything or anyone greater to validate an authentic word from God. The greatest freedom is having nothing to prove. If you truly have a word from God, it will not return void but will accomplish what God intends (Isa. 55:11).

Since I mentioned Jeremiah Johnson as a prophet who graciously climbed down, I should also share that I discovered a messianic Jew, Ron Cantor, who was given an unsought and surprising word when driving from Tel Aviv to Jerusalem that Joe Biden would be the next president. Cantor has produced evidence that he received this message in September 2020—some two months before the election. He did not forecast it widely, since he was counseled by leadership against it. Furthermore, Cantor, a staunch Republican, told me that he still voted for Trump! But this shows me that at least one person was trusted with a true secret from God during this memorable time. Why are there not more people like this? You tell me.

Level One: Holy Scripture

No prophetic word given since the closing of the canon of Scripture will be above or even equal to Holy Scripture. The

Bible is God's final revelation. No word given today is of the same level of authority or power as the Bible. Only a fool would claim to prophesy at the same level as that of those who wrote the sixty-six books of the Bible—thirty-nine in the Old Testament and twenty-seven in the New Testament.

Here is a most timely and sobering wisdom: "Every word of God proves true; he is a shield to those who take refuge in him. Do not add to his words, lest he rebuke you and you be found a liar" (Prov. 30:5–6). Never forget: God will not bend the rules for any of us.

Expository preaching is *not an embellishment* to Holy Scripture but rather explains, clarifies, and applies what is written. The preacher should aim to teach the Bible, to "expose" its truth, and to apply it with power and authority. God will honor that person who will teach and preach the Word without any effort to "improve" what is already written. Therefore, the prophet who claims to speak at the same level of Scripture is a false prophet.

Dear reader, if you want to get on the fast track to becoming yesterday's man or woman, underestimate the importance and the infallibility of the Bible.

The ancient Gnostics wormed their way into the early church by saying, "What you Christians teach is wonderful, but we can make it better." They nearly sank the church. When the writer of the epistle to the Hebrews said, "Jesus Christ is the same yesterday and today and forever," the writer of Hebrews purposefully and intentionally placed this verse right in the middle of a passage that stressed the perfection and permanence of the faith once for all given to the saints (Heb. 13:7–9). Not only is Jesus the same in his *person*, but he is also the same in what he taught. The New Testament affirms the Old Testament (2 Tim. 3:16; 2 Pet. 1:21) and Peter affirmed the teachings of the Apostle Paul (2 Pet. 3:15), showing that apostolic teaching is of the same level of authority as the Old Testament. It is *propositional* revelation, namely, "the" faith (Col. 2:7), "the" faith once for all delivered unto the saints (Jude 3).

I would urge you, reader, and especially all of those who have been entrusted with a unfeigned prophetic gift: Do not take this highest level of prophecy for granted. Let us remember the importance of God's Word! The psalmist said, "You have magnified your word above all your name" (Ps. 138:2, literal Hebrew translation).

The more you honor God's Word, the more he will honor you (1 Sam. 2:30).

Chapter 8

THE OATH AND
THE PROMISE

*For when God made a promise to Abraham, since he
had no one greater by whom to swear, he swore by
himself, saying, "Surely I will bless you and multiply
you." And thus Abraham, having patiently waited,
obtained the promise. For people swear by something
greater than themselves, and in all their disputes an
oath is final for confirmation. So when God desired to
show more convincingly to the heirs of the promise the
unchangeable character of his purpose, he guaranteed
it with an oath, so that by two unchangeable things, in
which it is impossible for God to lie, we who have fled for
refuge might have strong encouragement to hold fast to
the hope set before us.*

—HEBREWS 6:13–18

Put more trust in nobility of character than in an oath.

—SOLON (638–538 BC)

It is not the oath that makes us believe the man, but the man the oath.

—AESCHYLUS (525–456 BC)

"But I say to you, Do not take an oath at all."

—MATTHEW 5:34

His oath, his covenant, his blood,
Support me in the whelming flood;
When all around my soul gives way,
He then is all my hope and stay.
On Christ, the solid rock, I stand;
All other ground is sinking sand.

—EDWARD MOTE (1797–1874), "MY HOPE
IS BUILT ON NOTHING LESS"

Have you wondered what lay behind the Old Testament prophets who got it right when they prophesied? How could Elijah be so bold and so sure when he pronounced to King Ahab that there would not be a drop of rain until he said so (1 Kings 17:1)? How did Elijah remain calm on Mount Carmel in the face of hundreds of prophets of Baal, even making fun of them (1 Kings 18:20–40)?

Let me ask you a related question. Have you ever had a witness of the Spirit that *you know that you know that you know*? You were sure that you were not deceived, and you were not making this up. To put it another way, have you ever been so convinced of this witness of the Spirit that you were willing to stake your life on it a thousand times?

In my view, this is the experience of having God swear an oath to you. I call this type of confidence "oath-level assurance." It could also be called an "infallible assurance" (the Westminster Confession's language). Or it could be called the "immediate and direct" witness of the Holy Spirit (Dr. Martyn Lloyd-Jones's wording). This chapter is my contribution to a challenging topic.

I think Abraham experienced this assurance when he was willing to sacrifice Isaac (Gen. 22:16). And I believe this was what the writer of the book of Hebrews encouraged his readers to wait for and expect (Heb. 6:9–18).

I am convinced that oath-level assurance enables a person to "believe that you have received it" (Mark 11:24). This assurance gives you complete confidence that your prayer has been "heard" and that it will absolutely be answered (1 John 5:15).

Before I say more, I am not suggesting that people will get it right all the time. Some will be quick to say they experienced the oath yet still got their prediction wrong. It's helpful to remember that oath-level assurance has objective and subjective elements to it. Objectively speaking, the content may be verifiable; in the case of Elijah, it did not rain. Subjectively speaking, this assurance is something you believe in your heart, which cannot be empirically proven. It is critically important to have a balanced view of both of these elements in order to appropriately understand oath-level assurance.

Contemporary prophets bother people outside of the charismatic movement. These outsiders wonder why prophets today are acting like the prophets from the Old Testament.

Why do these prophets say "The Lord says" or "Thus says the Lord"? I too wish prophetic people would tone down invoking God's name when they teach. But here are two reasons prophetic people take on Old Testament mannerisms. First, they are aware of cessationist critiques, which deny that prophecy occurs today. For instance, the critics argue that if there were prophets today, they would not make mistakes. This critique makes prophetic people defensive and anxious to insist that they have got it right. Second, the prophets I got to know intimately would deny getting a word wrong. They would instead say that the word was wrongly applied. For example, I once asked Paul Cain whether he ever got it wrong. "No, I never have," he asserted with a straight face. However, I disagree with him. For example, Paul had told John Wimber, "Thus saith the Lord: revival will come to London." It did not. As I described earlier, Paul subsequently clarified, "I only said 'tokens' of revival." Throughout our friendship, I urged him again and again and again to stop saying, "Thus saith the Lord." Such explicit invoking of God's name is what people mean when they ask why prophetic people act like Old Testament prophets.

Now I am not saying God could not or would not raise up another prophet like Elijah or Nathan—I do not close the door on that possibility. But I think this would be rare. In my view, Paul Cain came close. Today some people claim this category for themselves, but I do not know who they are.

The secret to getting it right when you prophesy is absolutely knowing that God has sworn an oath to you. If one prophesies without first receiving this oath from God, he or she must expect to be on their own.

Let's consider Elijah. As I said, the absence of rain was an answer to his prayer. Scripture tells us Elijah prayed "fervently" that it would not rain (Jas. 5:17). Where did this idea come from? Was this God's idea? Was it Elijah's?

Elijah carried a burden for Israel because of the prevalence of Baal worship. Somehow, he came up with a way forward to defeat the enemy of the God of Israel—by praying that it would not rain. God fully assured Elijah that his prayer had been answered by swearing an oath to him. This gave Elijah confidence (one might call it a holy arrogance) before King Ahab to declare that there would not be a drop of rain "except by my word" (1 Kings 17:1).

Elijah only took orders from God, and God was the source of his power, "before whom I stand." Elijah's priority and motivation was the glory of the *God* of Israel, not patriotism. He was sold out to God, who had chosen Israel in the first place, and he understood God's ways.

If you are like me, I suspect oath-level assurance is new to you or at least is not common knowledge. In writing this chapter as well as in my ministry, I aim to know God's ways and invite others to seek him. God lamented that ancient Israel did not know his "ways" (Heb. 3:10), and this was part of the reason the people of Israel forfeited their inheritance (Heb. 3:18–4:1). Thus, even though it is important that prophets get confirmation from God for their words, all believers also need to thirst and hunger to know God's ways. It is my conviction that receiving an oath from God will make us who believe say with David (whatever your gift or calling), "The lines have fallen for me in pleasant places; indeed, I have a beautiful inheritance" (Ps. 16:6).

What Are the Differences between the Promise and the Oath?

Until recently, I did not fully appreciate the meaning of "two immutable things" in Hebrews 6:18 (KJV). The two immutable things are God's promise and his oath. Seeing this opened a new theological world for me. God initially gave a *promise* to Abraham that his seed would be as numerable as the stars in the heavens (Gen. 15:5). Some twenty years later God swore an *oath* to him that his seed would be as the stars in the heavens (Gen. 22:15–17). Both the promise and the oath were equally true, both of them were from God, and their *content* was exactly the same, namely, that Abraham's seed would be too many to count.

Why was there a need for this oath? I believe God swore the oath so we can know without a doubt that Abraham heard from him.

What is the difference between the promise and the oath?

One difference is the distinction between assurance and full assurance. Faith is assurance (Gr. *hypostasis*, Heb. 11:1). Faith is what justifies (Rom. 4:5). Faith is also seated in the heart (Rom. 10:9–10). But there is another word in the Greek, *plerophoria*, that refers to full assurance. This is the highest level of faith we can have during our pilgrimage here on earth. That is what Abraham finally experienced when he received the oath.

Another difference is that the swearing of an oath is more convincing than the promise alone. By swearing an oath God showed his promise "more convincingly" (Heb. 6:17). The oath makes the thing "very clear" (NIV). The New Living Translation emphasizes this point by translating it as "perfectly sure" (NLT). Abraham truly believed this initial promise, and his faith was counted for righteousness (Gen. 15:6). This belief in the promise became the Apostle Paul's scriptural basis for his teaching of justification by faith alone (Rom. 4).

Abraham *felt* the oath. The oath of God was utterly real and made God so real. After receiving God's oath, Abraham believed the same promise with a level of confidence that virtually amounted to having no doubt. It is not that he would never doubt, but the possibility of doubt was almost absent. God's voice to Abraham could have been physically audible or internally audible. Either way, Abraham was utterly and totally convinced that his seed would be innumerable, as if it already had happened.

Sometimes promises are conditional. One of the greatest promises of the Old Testament begins with "if":

"If my people who are called by my name humble themselves, and pray and seek my face and turn from their wicked ways, then I will hear from heaven and will forgive their sin and heal their land." (2 Chron. 7:14)

Likewise, the most famous verse in the New Testament has a condition:

"For God so loved the world, that he gave his only Son, that whoever believes in him should not perish but have eternal life." (John 3:16)

The promise of eternal life is offered on the condition "that whoever believes" shall receive eternal life.

The oath, however, is unconditional. Once God swears an

oath, it is irrevocable. Nothing—ever—can change it. There is nothing more wonderful than to have God swear an oath in mercy to you or me.

So when God swore the *oath* to Abraham, Abraham received an infallible assurance that his seed would *absolutely* and *irrevocably* be as the stars of the heavens and the sand on the seashore.

At the human-human level, an oath is more convincing than a promise. In the ancient world a promise might be broken, and this could be forgiven. But if one swore an oath, everyone would generally assume that the oath would be kept because the consequences were severe. If someone was caught breaking an oath, blood was shed.

Why do some require an oath today? Why does the president of the United States swear an oath on Inauguration Day? Why are people required to swear to tell "the whole truth and nothing but the truth" in a court of law?

The sad reality is, not everybody tells the truth! We live in a wicked world.

Some did say in ancient times that you could trust in one's nobility of character rather than an oath. A person with noble character could be believed without an oath. However, not all people have noble character, and this is why oaths are needed.

Examples of Human Oaths in the Bible

The Bible has examples of oaths made between people. It is important to see that even oaths made between wicked people have to be upheld because of the severe consequences involved in breaking an oath.

King Herod's Oath

Some seventeen hundred years after Abraham, on King Herod's birthday the daughter of Herodias danced before his guests. Herod was so pleased that he promised "with an oath" to give her whatever she might ask. Prompted by her mother, the daughter said, "Give me the head of John the Baptist here on a platter" (Matt. 14:6–8). This request upset the king.

Nevertheless, even wicked Herod kept his oath to have John the Baptist beheaded. We do not know whether the oath was connected to God's name or if Herod simply said, "I swear," but any oath in ancient times was respected. Therefore, because of his oath and the dinner guests watching, Herod ordered the death of John the Baptist (v. 9).

The Covenant Joshua Made with the Gibeonites

A covenant or treaty in the Ancient Near East was a mutual agreement between two parties equal in authority, and an oath was one part of putting the covenant into effect. By swearing an oath, the parties agreed to keep the terms of the covenant.

During the conquest of Canaan in Joshua 9, a group of people called the Gibeonites were well aware of how the Israelites kept their word. Because the Gibeonites foresaw that the Israelites would defeat everyone in Canaan, including them, they tricked Joshua into thinking they were also honest people. If they could convince Joshua that they were outsiders so the Israelites would make a covenant of peace with them, they would be safe (the NIV uses "treaty" and the ESV uses "covenant" to refer to the same thing). Once the terms of the covenant were agreed to, the covenant would be approved or ratified. Ratifying covenants involved swearing an oath to do or to refrain from doing what the covenantal agreement stated. In this case, Joshua and the Israelites swore an oath to let the Gibeonites live. Animal sacrifices accompanied such covenantal ceremonies to symbolize what would happen if one of the parties broke the terms of the covenant. If either party broke the covenant, the guilty party would suffer the same bloody fate as the sacrificed animal.

Joshua and the Israelites swore to let the Gibeonites live, putting the covenant into effect between the two groups (Josh. 9:15). However, the book of Joshua says that the Israelites did not seek the Lord on this matter (v. 14). And three days later Joshua found out he had been deceived. Did the Gibeonites' dishonesty and hypocrisy invalidate the force of the covenant? No. Joshua had sworn an oath to obey the covenant, and he had to live with his mistake for the rest of his life.

Several generations later, King Saul dishonored the covenant Joshua had made with the Gibeonites by killing some of them. There were no immediate consequences to Saul for his actions, but years later during King David's reign a famine came upon Israel that lasted three years. When David sought God's face to inquire about this famine, the Lord answered, "There is bloodguilt on Saul and on his house, because he put the Gibeonites to death" (2 Sam. 21:1). The famine did not happen because of something David had done. Rather, Saul had broken the covenant that Joshua and the people of Israel swore to keep. Even though both Joshua and Saul were dead, the covenant between the Israelites and the Gibeonites was still in force. Indeed, "Although the people of Israel had sworn to spare them [a few hundred years before], Saul had sought to strike them down in his zeal for the people of Israel and Judah" (v. 2). Because Saul failed to keep the oath of the covenant, atonement had to be made. David thus handed over seven of Saul's sons—an entire generation—to atone for Saul's mistake (vv. 8–9).

This shows how seriously God takes covenants and oaths made on the human level. One reason for this is because the people of Israel invoked God's name as a witness when they swore to obey the covenant. This brings another level of importance to human oaths: the name of the Lord. Israel could not take God's name lightly, and neither can we.

The Third Commandment

In the Sermon on the Mount, Jesus gave a new interpretation of three of the Ten Commandments. The sixth commandment is: You shall not murder (Matt. 5:21–26). A Pharisee would feel righteous in holding a grudge or remaining in unforgiveness as long as he had not physically murdered a person. But according to Jesus one committed murder if one was angry in his or her heart. The seventh commandment is: You shall not commit adultery (vv. 27–30). A Pharisee could indulge in pornography and not break the Law. But Jesus said that lusting or causing another to lust is adultery in the heart. The third commandment is: You shall not take the name of the Lord your God in vain (vv. 33–37). The original meaning of the third commandment is not merely referring to cursing or foul language, but is far deeper; it was given to guarantee truthfulness when bringing in God's holy name. Jesus applied this commandment so that people would never use God's name for personal benefit.

Jesus's application of the third commandment accomplished two things: First, it protected God's name by telling us *not to swear at all!* This meant we should never say, "The Lord told me." Thus, no one would be able to abuse God's name. Jesus knew too that if we bring in God's name we are not making *God* look good but *making ourselves look good.* So, you and I must always judge our words and ask, "Am I saying this to make God look good or to make me look good"? Second, Jesus wants us to tell the truth without having to appeal to something greater, whether heaven, earth, or Jerusalem (vv. 34–35). He stated that our conversation should be simply "Yes" or "No" (v. 37). In other words, I should simply tell the truth when I speak to you and should not have to say, "I swear I am telling you the truth." Some might say, "I swear by my mother's grave." One might say, "I cross my heart." I even have a friend who would say, "I swear by my love for Jesus." However, Jesus eliminates swearing altogether! Thus, although we do swear civil oaths in certain public settings, we cannot invoke God's name for our own self-interest.

James, the half brother of Jesus, followed Jesus's teaching in chapter 5 of the book of James. He turns his attention to a group of wealthy Christians in the Jerusalem church who had been withholding well-earned wages from helpless, poorer Christians. James warned these rich Christians that God in heaven has heard the "cries" of these poorer Christians and will vehemently judge these rich people (Jas. 5:1–5). At the same time, James turns to the poorer Christians and *warns them as well!* Even though James clearly comes down on the side of the poor, these mistreated Christians would be tempted to use James's name against these rich people—and point the finger at them. Their temptation would be to say, "See there, God is on our side and against you." However, James warns them that they should not do this or *they too* would be condemned. Then he quotes Jesus from the Sermon on the Mount:

> Do not swear, either by heaven or by earth or by any other oath, but let your "yes" be yes and your "no" be no, so that you may not fall under condemnation. (Jas. 5:12)

In other words, the workers in the field who had been financially abused were instructed not to claim that God was with them and against those rich Christians even though God *was* on their side and *against* the rich Christians! They were warned to leave God's name out entirely.

In general, people broke the third commandment when they used God's name to guarantee they were telling the truth when in fact they were not telling the truth. To say, "I swear by the name of the Most High God I am telling the truth" when in fact one was lying was to take God's name in vain. Another way they could break the third commandment was by swearing by the name of the Lord that they would keep their *vow*, or their end of a *covenant*, and then break it. And yet another way one could take the name of God in vain was when a prophet would say, "Thus says the LORD," when in fact that prophet had not been given such a mandate.

Take the prophet Hananiah as an example of one who abused the third commandment when he claimed that the children of Israel would be free from Babylonian captivity and back in Jerusalem in two years. He said, "Thus says the LORD of hosts, the God of Israel: I have broken the yoke of the king of Babylon. Within two years I will bring back to this place all the vessels of the LORD's house . . ." (Jer. 28:2ff). *Hananiah told the people what they wanted to hear.* This made him a very popular prophet.

On the other hand, Jeremiah was unpopular. First, he was accused of treason because he prophesied that the children of Israel would be taken to Babylon. It was thought that this could *never* happen to Israel—but Jeremiah's prophecy was right. Second, Jeremiah became even more hated because he prophesied that the captivity would last seventy years.

The people wanted to believe Hananiah's prophecy because he said that the captivity would last only two years. But Jeremiah confronted Hananiah: "Listen, Hananiah, the LORD has not sent you, and you have made this people trust in a lie." Jeremiah then prophesied to Hananiah: "[God] will remove you from the face of the earth. This year you shall die" (vv. 15–16). This word came to pass: "In that same year, in the seventh month, the prophet Hananiah died" (vv. 17).

Does God judge prophets today? Yes—but it is a mystery how this judgment happens. One possibility, as in the case of Hananiah, might be a prophet dying a premature death. Another possibility is that the Lord might permit open embarrassment to fall upon the false prophet who takes his name in vain, indefinitely covering that person with a cloud of doubt and suspicion.

Applying the Third
Commandment to Prophecy

Jesus's interpretation of the third commandment (Matt. 5:33–37) means that if I, R. T. Kendall, really do get a clear, undoubted, and direct word from God, I should not say so to you or to anyone else! God may turn on me if I break the confidence he has placed in me. If God should confide in me and reveal a secret (Ps. 25:14 KJV, NIV), I am not allowed to tell this, or even hint at this, to a living soul. Otherwise, *God may judge me.*

If I get a word from God for you, for example, I may say to you: "Here is what I believe you should think about . . ." then say it. I must not bring God's name in. Not at all. If my word "rings a bell" with you or turns out exactly as I predicted, you can conclude for yourself whether that word was from God. Do you see what I mean?

This is Jesus's own interpretation and application of the third commandment. We are all warned against the worst kind of "name-dropping"—using God's name to make ourselves look good. God will not have this.

What was so sad about the charismatic prophets' prediction of Trump's reelection was the way they would say, "The Lord says," "God told me," or "Thus says the Lord." Consider how this casts the name of the Most High God into the depths of the mud.

When I say to you, "Thus says the Lord," I am not making him look good; I am trying to elevate my credibility with you.

Listen! If God himself truly predicts something, it *will* come to pass! If someone says "Thus says the Lord" and it does not come to pass, this grieves God and makes him angry with whomever makes this claim.

The year 1956 was one of my best but also one of my worst years. It was a good year because the presence of the Lord was so real to me. I had visions and clear words from the Lord and was fully assured that God was with me and would even use me around the world. But it was one of my worst years because I lost my dad's and grandmother's approval, lost the support of virtually all my friends, and was forced to leave home. But the worst thing that happened during 1956 was when I broke the third commandment. I appealed to the Lord's name to prove I was in the right to my friends and relatives, saying that God himself had told certain things to me. To be honest, I believed God had indeed shown me things. But I should have kept quiet about this and should not have used his name to make myself appear spiritually mature to my dad.

There is no doubt that God spoke intimately with me in those days—but I couldn't keep quiet about it. My pride led me to tell my visions to people, and I was not making God look good. Not at all. But there is more. I misinterpreted many of those words, or visions (as I did with my dad when I tried to convince him how much God was with me). I certainly didn't make myself look good either!

You may ask: Why did God give me those words knowing that I would abuse them? I cannot be sure. This is almost like asking, "Why did God create humankind knowing we would suffer?" Answer: we won't know until we get to heaven. As to why God gave me visions which I misinterpreted, I don't know. Perhaps he let me make mistakes partly in order to teach me a little bit of humility. I *eventually* came to understand and appreciate many of these visions—as in the case of waiting for my father's approval for twenty-two years. Had I understood Jesus's interpretation of the third commandment in the Sermon on the Mount, I could have avoided a lot of pain and embarrassment.

This is why I am strongly convinced that you and I should think twice before we use language such as "the Lord told me" or seek to prophesy, "Thus saith the Lord." Many sincere people do this and have no idea they are breaking the third commandment. As I said, they use the Lord's name not to make God look good but, sadly, only to exalt themselves.

This, then, is partly why Jesus told us to let our conversation be simple by saying "Yes" or "No."

God Swears by His Own Name

I now return to the other main point of this chapter by examining Hebrews 6, which says that although it is not advisable for you or me to swear by God's name, God may still do so. *God himself* may swear an oath to us! "Since he had no one greater by whom to swear, he swore by himself" (Heb. 6:13).

Is there anything more amazing than this, that God would swear an oath to us? For example, in Genesis 22 God stepped in and unexpectedly swore an oath to Abraham, who was seconds away from sacrificing Isaac, the son of promise, according to God's command. STOP, God said: "Do not lay your hand on the boy or do anything to him, for now I know that you fear God, seeing you have not withheld your son, your only son, from me" (Gen. 22:12). Then he swore an oath to Abraham:

> "By myself I have sworn, declares the LORD, because you
> have done this and have not withheld your son, your only

son, I will surely bless you, and I will surely multiply your offspring as the stars of heaven and as the sand that is on the seashore." (vv. 16–17)

This historic moment is what the writer of Hebrews referred to: "For when God made a promise to Abraham, since he had no one greater by whom to swear, he swore by himself, saying, 'Surely I will bless you and multiply you'" (Heb. 6:13–14).

One could say that Abraham at this moment graduated from assurance of faith (Gr. *hypostasis*) to *full assurance* of faith (Gr. *plerophoria*).

When God swears an oath to someone, he or she has been blessed with the highest level of faith the Bible talks about—that is, on this side of heaven. However, Abraham did not receive this oath for a good while: he "patiently waited" for God to fulfill the promises he had initially made to him. It seems that God does not grant this high level of assurance very often.

If you want God to swear an oath to you, remember how the writer of Hebrews urged his Jewish Christian readers to persevere (Heb. 10:35). In line with this principle Abraham patiently waited, and after years of receiving promise after promise he finally obtained the ultimate reward from God. The example of Abraham is thus a sober reminder not to expect instantaneous maturity the day after one is saved. God could do this, of course! But the rule of thumb, if I may put it this way, is to be patient—to persevere and seek God's face with all your heart. Those who do this always find him true.

Before concluding this chapter, I need to bring up the two types of oaths God makes: oaths of mercy and oaths of judgment.

Oath of Mercy or Judgment

God may swear in mercy, as he did to Abraham (Heb. 6:13–14). This is the most wonderful thing that can happen to a Christian. The epistle to the Hebrews was written partly to encourage Jewish Christians to believe that God would swear an oath in mercy to them as he did to Abraham. These Hebrew Christians were very discouraged due to persecution and other troubles, but the writer encourages them and exhorts them. Having warned them of the possibility of falling away and being unable to repent again, he assures them of "better things" (v. 9) and then says:

> Do not throw away your confidence, which has a great reward. For you have need of endurance, so that when you have done the will of God you may receive what is promised. (Heb. 10:35–36)

When God swears an oath in mercy to us, it is a high affirmation from the Most High that he shares "secrets" and confides in us.

The opposite of this, however, is when God swears an oath in his anger, as he did to ancient Israel (Heb. 3:11). This is the worst thing that can happen to us. Such a situation is described in Hebrews 6:4–6, referring to those who had gone far in the things of God but had fallen away and could not be renewed again to repentance. These Christians had crossed over a line, like God's ancient people who had come out of Egypt and rebelled against him. Thus, they could no longer hear God speak, having become stone deaf to the Holy Spirit. I explain this situation in detail in

Are You Stone Deaf to the Spirit or Rediscovering God? (Christian Focus, UK).

I will now describe a few additional examples of God's oath swearing in the Old Testament.

Samuel, Eli, and Saul

Interestingly enough, the first official era of named prophets in the Old Testament which started with Samuel and his calling came out of an oath of judgment. God was angry with the house of Eli and told Samuel, "I swear to the house of Eli that the iniquity of Eli's house shall not be atoned for by sacrifice or offering forever" (1 Sam. 3:14). It must have been terrifying to hear God swear in his wrath. In a short period of time Eli's two sons Hophni and Phinehas, as well as Eli himself, died (1 Sam. 4:11, 18).

As for Samuel, God "let none of his words fall to the ground" (1 Sam. 3:19). That means everything Samuel prophesied came to pass: "All that he says comes true" (1 Sam. 9:6).

Samuel received another negative word later in his life, this time for King Saul. Saul had sinned by taking the ceremonial law lightly, offering a burnt offering against Moses' law (1 Sam. 13:9). Consequently, Samuel told Saul, "Your kingdom shall not continue" (v. 14). As a result of this deliberate disrespect for God's Word, Saul became yesterday's man (1 Sam. 16:1), even though he lived another twenty years. Saul eventually admitted, "God has turned away from me and answers me no more," before taking his own life (1 Sam. 28:15).

I need to give you a loving warning: a fast track to becoming yesterday's man is to go against God's teaching in Holy Scripture.

Elijah and Elisha

Elijah swore an oath to Ahab because God had sworn an oath to him: "As the LORD, the God of Israel, lives, before whom I stand, there shall be neither dew nor rain these years, except by my word" (1 Kings 17:1). All of this came true. Elijah also spoke with the same authority to the widow of Zarephath: "For thus says the LORD, the God of Israel, 'The jar of flour shall not be spent, and the jug of oil shall not be empty, until the day that the LORD sends rain upon the earth'" (v. 14). And so it turned out (v. 16).

And yet Elijah was very human, a man just like us (Jas. 5:17). Bold as a lion before the prophets of Baal, he became a pitiful coward when Jezebel vowed to get even with him. She used oath language: "So may the gods do to me and more also, if I do not make your life as the life of one of them by this time tomorrow" (1 Kings 19:2). However, her gods did not come through for her!

Elisha asked Elijah for a double portion of Elijah's anointing—and got it (2 Kings 2:9–12). It would seem that Elisha's request was fulfilled by comparing the number of miracles. You could count around seven miracles in Elijah's ministry, but twice as many in Elisha's era. It was even said that Elisha could tell what a foreign king spoke in his own bedroom (2 Kings 6:12).

The Oath for You and Me

Does this mean if you received an oath from God that this would make you another Elijah or Elisha? No. Not all who come into full assurance of faith receive a gift of prophecy, much less a gift like what the prophets of the Old Testament had. Never forget that the Elijahs and Nathans of this world were rare back then, and will most certainly always be rare. But for anyone to proceed to prophesy without having the same kind of relationship with God like these men had is to guarantee huge disappointments, if not disasters.

I pray that I am wrong, but I fear that so many of today's prophets who use "Thus says the Lord" language are too much like the Hananiahs of this world, telling people what they hope will be true. Some of these prophets do not differentiate between their personal wish and God's infallible judgment.

I believe Hebrews 6:13–20 is a *promise* that God can actually *swear an oath* to you and me, as he did to Abraham. This is a promise worth holding on to, an experience worth waiting for. After Abraham patiently endured, he "obtained the promise"— that is, the *promise of the oath* (v. 15). For Abraham, this meant experiencing God's oath directly and immediately. Thankfully, this experience is for us too.

If you believe you have a high-level prophetic calling, I urge you to seek God's face so that he can swear an oath to you before you give a prophetic word. And then leave God's name out in your prophecies. You will never be sorry if you leave his name out. If the prophecy comes true, let others say, "That was the Lord." If it does not come true, at least you have not said, "The Lord told me."

After you finish reading this chapter, please remember that one of the purposes of the letter to the Hebrews is that you and I might experience what Abraham experienced: having God swear an oath in mercy to us. Oath-level assurance is what Old Testament prophets like Elijah experienced.

How do you know if you have received the oath? I answer:

you will know. This is what lay behind Jesus's words: "Whatever you ask in prayer, believe that you have received it, and it will be yours" (Mark 11:24). This is also what the Apostle John meant when he explained that we can *know* when we have prayed in the will of God, therefore receiving answers to our prayers (1 John 5:14–15). This is oath-level assurance.

If we want a close relationship with God, we need to seek his face for full assurance about what we believe, how we pray, and what we prophesy. This will save us a lot of embarrassment, because God will honor us. And then we will bring honor to him.

Chapter 9

IS GOD JUDGING THE
CHURCH TODAY?

*"For the Lord GOD does nothing
without revealing his secret
to his servants the prophets."*

—AMOS 3:7

*"Behold the days are coming," declares the
Lord GOD,
"when I will send a famine on the land—
not a famine of bread, nor a thirst for water,
but of hearing the words of the LORD.
They shall wander from sea to sea,
and from north to east;
they shall run to and fro, to seek the word of
the LORD,
but they shall not find it."*

—AMOS 8:11–12

"The LORD has put a lying spirit in the mouth of all these your prophets; the LORD has declared disaster for you."

— 1 KINGS 22:23

My greatest fear is that the Lord would take his hand off me.

— BILLY GRAHAM (1918–2018)

I honestly believe that some in the prophetic wing of the charismatic movement are under the judgment of God. I believe God sent a lying spirit to the prophets who said that Donald Trump would have two consecutive terms in the White House. Where did I get this idea? Could it have come from God? Maybe—you tell me. But I want you to consider this possibility as a reasonable explanation of why virtually all of these prophets led so many sincere Christians to believe that Donald Trump would be president for another four years.

I am not a prophet. I am a Bible teacher, although my friend Michael Eaton used to call me a "holiness preacher." I am not so arrogant to think I have the final word, and I would never claim that God writes my books or prepares my sermons. All my books, including this one, get edited because it is important to receive input from others. My longtime friend from London, Lyndon Bowring, went over many sermons with me before I preached. Even after I delivered the sermons, he lovingly criticized them! Additionally, Dr. Martyn Lloyd-Jones vetted virtually everything I preached during my first four years at Westminster Chapel. I give these examples to prove that I am not above criticism. And people making bold predictions in God's name should also seek to receive healthy criticism from others.

I have come close to making prophetic statements at least three times. I already have told you about the first time, when in 1992 I called the charismatic movement Ishmael and mentioned that Isaac—the next Great Awakening—would be coming. I consider my second prophetic statement to be when I said America is under God's judgment in my recent book, *We've Never Been This Way Before*. And, finally, this volume, *Prophetic Integrity*, feels very similar to these other two instances.

What I Would Go to the Stake For

I would go to the stake for saying that open theism is the most dangerous teaching that has ever entered the church. I am also convinced that it is particularly treacherous for the charismatic movement. The prophetic movement has been combining the teachings of open theism with the prosperity gospel. Prophets see themselves as instrumental in making things happen and are naming and claiming this or that in the name of the Lord.

Open theism, which I will fully define later, has been championed by liberals seeking to undermine the Bible. That's why I refer to it as theological liberalism. This teaching has destroyed the faith of countless evangelicals. For example, my professor Dale Moody (1915–1992), whom I studied under at Southern Baptist Seminary from 1970–72, once publicly declared, "I went from fundamentalism (belief in the infallibility of the Bible) to Karl Barth (1886–1968), a universalist, from Barth to Paul Tillich (1886–1965), who called God 'the ground of all being,' and from Tillich to process theology, and now I don't know where I am."

Open theism has now gone forth from the academy and

infiltrated many churches; a prominent teacher from Fuller Theological Seminary introduced it into the charismatic movement several years ago. Many people who embrace open theism have not heard the term, nor do they realize they have been largely controlled by it. This aberrant theology is deadly. It is poison. It is a cancer. Sooner or later it will make fools of those who don't see through it and reject it.

Give me a moment to share my heart about this matter. Never in my life have I felt so helpless, heavy, and awkward yet sure in my writing as in this chapter. Here is the problem: Although I will not mention names or locations, I will refer to the *theology* of some admired Christian leaders, some of whom happen to be among my closest friends. Some of them endorsed my books, and I some of theirs. Not only that, I believe that they love the Lord as much as I do, maybe more.

On different occasions over the years, people have disagreed with me and added, "There's nothing personal in this, R. T., I love you very much." I believed them. My own dad sits at the top of a list of such people. I hope I show to you, the reader, but also to *them* that this chapter is the exact same scenario: there is nothing personal in what I say.

Jesus told his close friend Simon Peter on one occasion, "Get behind me, Satan!" That did not mean Peter was demon-possessed or that he was permanently ensnared in an irrevocable deception. It did mean that Peter was at that time a "hindrance" to Jesus, temporarily focusing *not* on "the things of God, but on the things of man" (Matt. 16:23). I choose to believe this is the explanation regarding those who uphold some of the teachings I will mention shortly. I do not want you to try to figure out who said this or that or who holds to this or that way of thinking. Indeed, I pray that you will never know who taught this or that. My hope is rather that you will *recognize and reject* these false *teachings*. That is what matters—not who taught this or that but *what* needs to be detected and destroyed.

Two Dangerous Deficiencies

In my observation, charismatics generally have two deficiencies. First, many have *no theology of suffering*. They completely ignore numerous plain Scriptures in the New Testament. For example, Jesus said we would suffer: "In the world you will have tribulation. But take heart; I have overcome the world" (John 16:33). He also told the church of Smyrna, "Do not fear what you are about to suffer" (Rev. 2:10). Peter and John rejoiced that they were "counted worthy to suffer dishonor for the name" (Acts 5:41). Paul reckoned that "the sufferings of this present time are not worth comparing with the glory that is to be revealed to us" (Rom. 8:18). Finally, Paul also noted that it has been "granted" that we should not only believe in the Lord "but also suffer for his sake" (Phil. 1:29).

Second, many charismatics lack any theology of divine judgment upon Christians; that is, they do not teach that God can step in to judge the church and his people. However, Jesus once said to the church of Ephesus that "unless you repent" he himself would "remove your lampstand from its place" (Rev. 2:5). Additionally, the early church fundamentally held to the doctrine of chastening, or disciplining. The Lord chastens and disciples those whom he loves (Heb. 12:6). Chastening, in fact, is essentially God judging us. I would thus ask those who say,

"If Paul the apostle had my faith, he would not have his thorn in the flesh," does God not chasten his people today? Indeed, chastening and divine judgment are used interchangeably (see 1 Cor. 11:32).

Jesus Christ is the same yesterday, today, and forever (Heb. 13:8). If we could see him, he would look the same (same face, same nail prints in his hands); he loves the same individuals (we are loved with an everlasting love); he disciplines the same way (to show we are true children and not illegitimate); and he warns the same people (because he has not deserted us).

When I read Amos's word, "For the Lord GOD does nothing without revealing his secret to his servants the prophets" (Amos 3:7), I ask: Is this still true? Or are we in the era of which Amos spoke, a famine of "hearing the words of the LORD" (Amos 8:11)? That means that God says *nothing*. A famine of hearing the word of the Lord would come for one reason: as a sign of God's *silent* judgment.

In my recent book, *We've Never Been This Way Before*, I wrote about five types of judgment: retributive, gracious, redemptive, natural, and silent. In this chapter, I talk most about God's silent judgment. God's silent judgment is the worst kind—it is so scary. When God is this angry, he does nothing or says nothing but suddenly reveals his anger without warning. God is not like you and me; we tend to easily and quickly show our anger. But the angrier God is, the longer he waits to show it. For example, God suddenly rained fire and brimstone on Sodom and Gomorrah without any warning after waiting a long time for them to repent (Gen. 19). There are two ways that Amos develops the idea of silent judgment. First, God is showing love and attention when he warns his prophets in advance. Second, when there is a famine of hearing the word of the Lord, we don't know what he is thinking; we can only beg him for mercy.

It seems very ominous indeed that COVID-19 took not only the world but the church by utter surprise. The earliest message of the New Testament was that of John the Baptist, who said to his Pharisee and Sadducee hearers, "Who warned you to flee from the wrath to come?" (Matt. 3:7). Did anybody warn them? Or was there no warning until John said this?

Today, there are two kinds of prophets that warn people. The first kind is those who do not go by the name of "prophet," but whose understanding of Holy Scripture leads them to warn people in authority. They speak with such authority as if they heard directly from God, and I do believe that some of them are cessationists. I caution you not to dismiss these people just because they may be cessationists, since their words still proclaim the truth. I am not a cessationist, so I would like to believe that this book in general, and this chapter in particular, is a bit prophetic. I make no claim that the Lord told me what to write in this book! But I would go to the stake for what I affirm in this book.

The second type of prophet is those whose revelatory gifts have the seal and approval of the Most High God, the God of the Bible. I hope that they minister among us. I said in chapter 7 that I do not rule out the possibility that noncanonical prophets like Nathan or Elisha exist today. There are almost certainly people around who would claim this.

Here is my question: Why would some of this second type of prophetic people be able to call out the names and addresses of men and women from vast audiences but not warn that a pandemic was at hand? How does it have any *value* to the world, and to the church of God, when prophets can reveal a person's name and date of birth but not foresee the emergence of a global pandemic, outbreaks of violence, the destruction of neighborhoods by fire, disunity, the racism shown by the horrible death of George Floyd (1973–2020), or the violent attack on the United States Capitol building by those disputing the presidential election?

God knew all of these tragic events were coming. Did God tell these prophets? Why didn't they tell us?

America under Judgment?

I am truly afraid God is angry with us. I fear the present moment is similar (in some ways) to when God poured out his wrath upon Sodom and Gomorrah. Instead of fire and brimstone, however, we have been afflicted by COVID-19 and widespread fear. Fear? Would God actually bring fear? Yes. For example, God warned Israel that if they did not turn back to him, he would inflict a "trembling heart" and "a languishing soul" upon them. "Night and day you shall be in *dread* and have no assurance of your life. In the morning you shall say, 'If only it were evening!' and at evening you shall say, 'If only it were morning!' because of the *dread that your heart shall feel*" (Deut. 28:65–67, emphasis mine). God is a jealous God.

It is my fear that God is angry with America because she has not maintained her early choice to honor him. The early Puritans were men and women whose solid belief in the Bible gave them courage to move to America. Boston was founded by the Puritan leader John Winthrop (1588–1649). Connecticut was founded by the Puritan minister Thomas Hooker (1586–1647). Harvard University (founded in 1636) and Yale University (founded in 1701) were established by people who were governed by the fear of God. There is a difference between Israel and America: God chose Israel, but America chose God. America's choice to be a nation under God is demonstrated in the Declaration of Independence, the Constitution, the references to God on our money, the holiday of Thanksgiving Day, the historic references to the Ten Commandments in connection with the Supreme Court, the fact that Congress begins every day with prayer, and the explicit reference to God in our patriotic hymns—for a start!

Our choosing God does not mean we are a theocracy—no, not at all. But we took God seriously. After all, "Blessed is the nation whose God is the LORD" (Ps. 33:12). "Righteousness exalts a nation, but sin is a reproach to any people" (Prov. 14:34). Although we have never been a theocracy, America inherited many of the fringe benefits that described Israel when they put God first. Any such nation would prosper and be the "head and not the tail" (Deut. 28:13). Our nation continually won wars and expanded for a long time. However, around the time of the Vietnam War (1955–1975) we began losing confidence and started to experience crises and setbacks. One could say that we stopped winning.

Pinpointing precisely where and when we began to drift is not my expertise. But I am sure that at some point we effectively said to God, "We no longer want you." And God heard this. As I state in my book, *We've Never Been This Way Before*, America is under judgment not only for societal sins like racism and immorality, but especially for the theological liberalism in our pulpits.

Theological liberalism used to refer only to those who denied the inspiration of the Bible, the deity of Jesus Christ, the virgin birth, Jesus's resurrection from the dead, the need to be saved, the second coming, and the final judgment. These people and ideas remained, for the most part, in universities and seminaries. But a new kind of liberalism has now emerged among evangelicals and charismatics alike. The irony is, you can hold to many biblical teachings and feel that this is sufficient for you to be "sound" in doctrine. But this new liberalism is a *blend*; it is a mixture of old wine and new wine. The old wine is historic Christianity. The new wine is teachings that used to be regarded as sheer heresy.

Open Theism

The new liberalism to which I refer is undergirded by open theism. Bear with me if you feel this is out of your depth; I will be simple. The premise of open theism is that God's knowledge of the future is not predetermined and, therefore, *needs us* for input. God cannot do anything without us. This view holds that there are many futures and God does not know which future will happen. Open theism thus reduces God to a contingency planner because he knows every possibility but does not know which path his creation—you and I—will choose. This teaching is a spin-off from process theology, which is pantheism—the view that all is God. Some open theists would want to be disassociated from pantheism, so they call their position panentheism—all is in God. Nevertheless, open theism is really process theology in evangelical dress. Many holding to these views still believe in the virgin birth and resurrection of Jesus, and even affirm the second coming. I cannot say how they would preach on the danger of missing heaven when we die or how they hold that people could spend eternity consciously in hell. Many of them are even universalists. Yet they claim biblical support for their teachings.

As I mentioned earlier in this chapter, I suspect most lay people who are open theists have never heard the term, nor would they be able to define their beliefs. I will soon give a list of twenty propositions. These teachings are either spawned by open theist premises or merely cohere with them (even if accidentally).

I come to you, dear reader, on bended knee to ask whether your own faith resonates with any of the following propositions? If so, I lovingly caution you: you have—even if unknowingly—almost certainly departed from Holy Scripture as it has been generally interpreted for two thousand years. To repeat the wine analogy I just made, some who uphold these troubling perspectives would call what I teach "old wine." They might say the teachings I will critique are "new wine," which must not be poured into old wineskins lest the skins burst!

History is repeating itself. The biggest danger to the early church, after all, was not persecution but false teaching creeping in.

It is written, "Jesus Christ is the same yesterday and today and forever" (Heb. 13:8). This statement refutes two things: (1) it refutes cessationism, as I have said before, but also (2) open theism, the view that the future is unknown by God. Hebrews 13:8 is deliberately set between Hebrews 13:7 and Hebrews 13:9 to ensure that *the* faith remains the same. We need to uphold "the" faith once for all delivered to the saints (Jude 3). It is not "a" faith but "the faith" (Col. 2:7). This faith is eternal and unchanging. It is indeed propositional revelation, which means that the Christian faith is based on eternal truths that can be put into propositions. For example, Jesus was born of a virgin; God is a jealous God; God is sovereign, omniscient (all-knowing), and omnipotent (all-powerful); the blood of Jesus satisfies God's justice; and justification by faith alone is what saves us. However, propositional revelation is rejected by liberals and, more importantly for this book, charismatic open theists.

Twenty Faulty Propositions and My Response

Twenty propositions *in italics* follow, which I hope you will instantly reject. These propositions are examples of what many, sadly, teach today. I am not saying that all open theists endorse every one of these propositions, but with this list I hope to show you how to identify what is false and uphold the truth about God. Following each faulty proposition I show exactly why, in my heart-of-hearts opinion, it is wrong.

1. *If your purpose in prayer is not to change God's will, you are wasting your time.*

   My reply: This perspective suggests that the purpose of prayer is to manipulate God for our purposes rather than to know him. The truth is, time in prayer is never wasted time. You get to know *anyone's* ways by spending time with this person. It is the same with God—he loves your company. Time with God increases your sense of his presence. "In all your ways acknowledge him, and he will make straight your paths" (Prov. 3:6).

2. *God is in charge, but not in control. He left us in control.*

    My reply: This makes us more important than God. On the contrary, Jesus is at the right hand of God upholding the universe by his power (Heb. 1:3). Woe unto all of us if we are in control! Instead, thank God that Jesus is in control.

3. *God does not approach the world with the idea of imposing his will on it.*

    My reply: It was by the will of God that we were created in his image—male and female (Gen. 1:27). He also gave specific commands to Adam from the beginning. Additionally, "Of his own will he brought us forth by the word of truth, that we should be a kind of firstfruits of his creatures" (Jas. 1:18).

4. *Like a good earthly father, our heavenly Father would never use hardship and persecution to bring his children closer to himself.*

    My reply: On the contrary, "the Lord disciplines the one he loves, and chastises every son whom he receives" (Heb. 12:6). The Greek word for "chastises" ("scourges," KJV) means to whip with thongs. God, then, does what it takes to bring us to submission when we go off the rails.

5. *Nothing happens without declaration. Unless I declare or claim this or that to happen, nothing will ever happen.*

149

My reply: God answers prayer beyond "all that we ask or think, according to the power at work within us" (Eph. 3:20). God hears prayer that is according to his will (1 John 5:14); therefore, what we may declare or ask for must be under his leadership. Isn't it amazing how God also gives us things we did not ask for?

6. *We have been given the job of transforming the world. This job is doable and is doable before Jesus gets back.*

    My reply: Our job is to share the gospel with every person (Matt. 28:19; Mark 16:15). If the world were transformed before Jesus comes, why is it written that Jesus will "execute judgment on all," showing that ungodly people will be around (Jude 14–15). Indeed, Jesus will come with his mighty angels "in flaming fire, inflicting vengeance on those who do not know God and on those who do not obey the gospel of our Lord Jesus" (2 Thess. 1:8).

7. *God wants everyone to be healed; if you are not healed, it is due to your lack of faith.*

    My reply: This teaching has driven sincere people to despair, blaming themselves for their own continued sickness or for the death of loved ones. But Jesus never— ever—scolded a person for not being healed. Why some are healed and others are not lies within the mystery of God's sovereignty (Exod. 33:19). No one has perfect faith, and not all pray the prayer of faith as in James 5:15. Besides, we all will eventually die.

8. *Anything negative is of Satan; God would never cause calamity or a pandemic.*

   My reply: People believe this statement not because they value Scripture but only because they *want* to believe this and *choose* to hope this is true. However, it is utterly without biblical foundation since God is on record as saying, "I make well-being and create calamity" (Isa. 45:7) and "I will turn your feasts into mourning" (Amos 8:10). Even Jesus himself says to the church of Thyatira that he will throw a false prophetess "onto a sickbed, and those who commit adultery with her I will throw into great tribulation" (Rev. 2:22).

9. *We should not honor the martyrs the way they have often been honored. The early church meant well, but now we understand that martyrdom is a failure of the church to pray. Stephen should never have been stoned (Acts 7:59–60).*

   My reply: God himself honors the martyrs. "I saw under the altar the souls of those who had been slain for the word of God . . . they were each given a white robe" (Rev. 6:9, 11). Those who were "beheaded" for the testimony of Jesus were given special recognition (Rev. 20:4). Stephen, in fact, was rewarded by seeing Jesus "standing" at the right hand of God during his martyrdom (Acts 7:56). Some did escape "the edge of the sword," but others were "stoned" or "sawn in two" (Heb. 11:34, 37). Nevertheless, "all these" were equally "commended" for their faith (v. 39).

10. *The death of Ananias and Sapphira was an abuse of apostolic authority.*

My reply: This blasphemous notion accuses Peter of manipulating the Spirit to kill Ananias and Sapphira for their deceitfulness, as if an apostle could make God do this. However, God did do this, and he may do this again if we enter a true revival situation like what the early church experienced. "Great fear" consequently came upon everyone, and this brought such respect that no outsider "dared join" the believers (see Acts 5:7–11, 13).

11. *God changes his plans every day, depending on how we prayed the day before.*

My reply: This is a typical way an open theist thinks. The implication is that God has no will of his own; rather, he looks to us for input to know what to do next. This is the logical conclusion one makes if God does not know the future. The Bible says, however, that God does knows what will happen: "My counsel shall stand, and I will accomplish all my purpose" (Isa. 46:10). Indeed, God works all things "according to the counsel of his will" (Eph. 1:11).

12. *What is the will of God? On earth as it is in heaven: if no sickness exists there, it should not exist here.*

My reply: For centuries Christians believed that the petition in the Lord's Prayer, "Your will be done, on earth as it is in heaven" (Matt. 6:10), meant that as there is no rebellion in heaven, so we too submit to whatever God's will for us is. But given the logic of the open theist proposition, you could also say, "There is no death in heaven; therefore we should not die," which is not true.

13. *The Bible is only a rough guide. We need to go off the edges of the map to find new ways to experience the supernatural power of God.*

My reply: This statement is a dead giveaway that one expressing such ideas is arbitrarily deciding not to be led entirely by Scripture. This is the most dangerous thing of all. The ancient Gnostics thought this way: "We can make Christianity better." However, when someone departs from Scripture to find new ways to experience the supernatural, this person is vulnerable to the power of Satan—an angel of light (2 Cor. 11:14).

14. *We can't camp around old truth. We need new truth.*

My reply: If it is "new" truth, it is not true. This would mean that the Bible is not good enough. As we saw earlier, the consequence of Jesus Christ being the same yesterday and today and forever is that true doctrine does not change (Heb. 13:7–9). "For I the LORD do not change" (Mal. 3:6). God's Word is "forever" and "firmly fixed in the heavens" (Ps. 119:89). We may have fresh insights into truth, but the truth of God does not change.

15. *If the Apostle Paul had the faith that he should have had, he would not have had his thorn in the flesh. A thorn in the flesh could never come from God.*

My reply: We don't know what Paul's "thorn" was, as I say in my book *Thorn in the Flesh*. But it was a painful nuisance. Paul needed this thorn to keep him from becoming conceited or admired too highly. He did pray three times that God would take it away (2 Cor. 12:8), but God replied: "My power is made perfect in weakness" (v. 9). I will welcome God's response, too! The truth is, if all of us are honest, we have things in our lives that are painful but won't leave. Or is there anyone among us who does not struggle with an ego problem?

16. *The Bible's prophecies are conditional, and we can change them.*

    My reply: *Some* prophecies are conditional (e.g. 2 Chron. 7:14; John 3:16). But not many of them are. For example, the prophecies about the Messiah were not conditional. Jesus arrived "when the fullness of time had come" (Gal. 4:4), which shows that God decided exactly when the eternal Word would become flesh. When God decides the time when his Son will return, he will come whether we are *ready or not* (Matt. 24:45–51).

17. *Jesus is returning for a glorious bride, one who has fulfilled his mandate to go to all the earth and disciple nations until the world looks like heaven.*

    My reply: The world will never look like heaven unless God by his own power makes this happen. The earth groans in travail awaiting the day God himself changes it (Rom. 8:22). A great awakening may precede the second coming, but not all will be saved. There are still some things that await glorification (Rom. 8:30), when we shall all be "changed" (1 Cor. 15:51). It has been an unchangeable truth from the beginning that not all will be saved; those who do find what is offered are "few" (Matt. 7:14).

18. *Disregard the book of Job; God does not want any of us to go through what Job endured.*

    My reply: Who is to say what God may choose for some of us? God is the one—not Satan—who instigated the long ordeal that Job went through (Job 1:8). This book has been a priceless treasure for centuries for those who have endured great heartache, financial reverse, and physical suffering. And, best of all, Job learned what we all need to learn: "I know that you can do all things, and that no purpose of yours can be thwarted" (Job 42:2).

19. *Our world is not deteriorating; it is advancing. Things are getting better. The world will sooner or later look like heaven—even before Jesus comes back.*

    My reply: Where did anyone get information like this? The Bible says that people will go from "bad to worse" (2 Tim. 3:13), yet this is being taught! The idea that "things are getting better" was the view of old-fashioned postmillennialism a hundred years ago, which died with the coming of World War I. And even more recently millions have died from the COVID-19 pandemic. I cannot imagine how people can say things are getting better.

20. *The purpose of prayer is not to accept God's will, but to change it.*

My reply: If anyone could have changed God's will, Jesus would have done it. He asked if there might be any way he could avoid the cup he was destined to drink (Luke 22:42). Jesus is thus our example. Any child of God might indeed *ask* God to let us avoid suffering. Jesus did. Paul did. I have done so many times. But true devotion is to dignify God's trials. We are to count it pure joy when these trials happen and not complain (Jas. 1:2).

At first glance you may find some of these propositions bizarre or reprehensible. But once you accept *even one* of these precepts, it is only a matter of time before you find more and more of them appealing. I believe the twenty statements I just outlined are a fulfillment of Jesus's warnings that there would be false prophets in the last days who would seek "to lead astray, if possible, even the elect" (Matt. 24:24).

I am *not* saying that if a person believes any one of these propositions he or she is not saved. Neither am I saying that if someone believes *all* of these propositions he or she is an irrevocably false prophet. I prefer to believe that people teaching these things have been overtaken *temporarily* in a *theological fault* and that our Christian duty is to try to restore such people in a spirit of meekness, while diligently guarding ourselves lest we also temporarily give in to teaching we should later renounce (Gal. 6:1).

And yet, if I am totally honest, I will go on record to say that I would not want to be in the shoes of any single person who believes or teaches those twenty statements. *The Lord has told me nothing* about people who believe these ideas. But I can say one thing for sure: it is only a matter of time before those who hold to these views will end up having deep, deep regret.

If you hold to these views yet have a change of mind before it is too late, this change will likely come after I am in heaven. It would be a satisfying legacy if this book in general and the present chapter in particular does some good.

I earnestly pray that the tone of this book comes through to you. I write in unfeigned love and genuine concern for the future of the body of Christ. I said earlier that some of my friends hold to these views and are aware of this book being published. I care about them and we pray for each other every day, but I am still deeply concerned for them.

I am convinced that the views in these propositions are unbiblical. Indeed, I believe God is angry with both evangelical and charismatic open theists. As Jesus turned the tables upside down in the temple because of the Father's disapproval (John 2:14–16) and as he spoke to the church of Thyatira from the right hand of God with eyes like a flame of fire (Rev. 2:18), so I too believe God is judging *all of us* in the church today.

It is wrong when people are ecstatic over a prophet calling one's name out of a congregation of thousands but are not interested in prophets who are chosen by the Holy Spirit to warn America about the present crises we face. The prophets who predicted Donald Trump's election were unable to make the distinction between what they personally hoped for and what God had decided in advance. After all, God Almighty put Joe Biden in the White House (Rom. 13:1–7; Ps. 75:6–8). Never forget that Nero was emperor of Rome when Paul commanded us to pray for kings and all who are in high positions and when Peter said, "Honor the emperor" (1 Tim. 2:2; 1 Pet. 2:17).

God once sent a "lying spirit in the mouth of all [Ahab's] prophets" (1 Kings 22:22). Please pray that I am wrong that this event was being repeated when nearly all the prophets predicted Biden's defeat. Why did God send the lying spirit? Because he was angry. Very angry. So much so that it is recorded: "The LORD has declared disaster for you" (v. 23). Disaster? Yes. Away with the notion that God does not do this sort of thing!

If I decide that God can do only what I consider good and that Satan is behind what does not seem good to me, it is because I *choose* to believe that. But this is not the plain and clear teaching of the Bible.

The church of Thyatira angered God, but there were faithful exceptions there who did not follow false teaching (Rev. 2:24). Ezekiel prophesied that judgment upon the people of Jerusalem was a certainty because of their sins against God. Although men like Daniel, Noah, and Job could be spared individually, such holy lives would not thwart the judgment to come (Ezek. 14:14).

Likewise, there are millions of charismatics who love God and walk in godliness. There are millions of evangelicals who love God and walk in godliness. However, such numbers may not be enough to avert God's judgment.

I'm sorry, but it is my opinion that God has judged prophetic people left, right, and center. What other explanation is there for how they got it so wrong with the 2020 presidential election and missed seeing the greatest natural disaster of our generation?

Billy Graham said that his greatest fear was that God would take his hand off him. This kind of humility is sorely needed today. I feel that God has judged the church merely by taking his hand off us. It has been said many times, "If the Holy Spirit were completely taken from the church today, ninety percent of the work of the church would continue as if nothing had happened." This shows how complacent people have become.

And yet I am *not* saying that the Holy Spirit has completely withdrawn from the church. But I will say what I think is pretty well accepted: The common denominator of many charismatics and possibly also Pentecostals today is prosperity teaching. Fifty years ago the thread that held charismatics and Pentecostals together was largely the gifts of the Holy Spirit, especially healing. But it seems that when fewer and fewer people were being healed, as some of the television evangelists experienced, the emphasis shifted to prosperity teaching. These new teachings cohered with the "What's in it for me?" question motivating many people. Sadly, the question "What's in it for God?" is hardly asked these days.

My fear is that the church in the United States is too preoccupied with politics. And this focus on politics is replacing the urgency for soul winning and saving the lost. Churches are not growing as they once were, and the percentage of people who believe Jesus Christ is the only way to heaven is decreasing every year.

Has God taken his hand off the church? I fear that he has. Please pray that I am wrong. If God has taken his hand off the church, I hope it is temporary. It is my view that the same Jesus described in the book of Revelation, having eyes like a "flame of fire" and showing his anger (Rev. 2:18), is looking at us now. But it is equally true that God warns because there is still hope. Jesus rebukes and warns those whom he loves (Rev. 3:19).

My hope, therefore, is this: If God's silent judgment was what lay behind the failure of the people of God to be warned of the COVID-19 pandemic, it is my prayer and hope that his silent judgment will be paralleled by his gracious judgment, serving as a wake-up call to change us. This means there is still hope. The disasters of our day are God's call to get our attention so that we will fall upon our knees in repentance.

Chapter 10

PROPHETIC INTEGRITY

A Call for Honesty, Vulnerability, and Repentance

"But I have this against you, that you have abandoned the love you had at first. Remember therefore from where you have fallen; repent, and do the works you did at first. If not, I will come to you and remove your lampstand from its place, unless you repent. Yet this you have: you hate the works of the Nicolaitans, which I also hate."

—Revelation 2:4–6

The church right now has more fashion than passion, is more pathetic than prophetic, is more superficial than supernatural.

—Leonard Ravenhill (1907–1994)

There is hope. Hope is realistic expectancy.

You might be surprised that I believe that God's silent judgment will be paralleled by his gracious judgment despite the darkness all around us, as I mentioned at the close of the previous chapter. God did not warn us about COVID-19. No prophet, no politician, no billionaire, no Christian, and no Muslim can get credit for saying, "I told you so." However, God's gracious judgment with over 900,000 deaths so far in the United States alone has yet to awaken us. We have not changed. Some Christians are already focusing on the next presidential election in 2024. At the time of my writing this book, our questions are trivial: "When will life be normal again? When can we go watch football and baseball in person or go to our favorite restaurants without worrying about COVID-19 protocols?"

Would another pandemic, but ten times worse than COVID-19, wake us up? I am afraid it would not, unless it is accompanied by the effectual call of the Holy Spirit. The COVID-19 wake-up call has not changed us. The violence in cities that occurred at the same time has not changed us.

I thought we would change after September 11, 2001. After the planes crashed in New York, in Pennsylvania, and near Washington, D.C., a feeling of comradery appeared. There was a temporary increase in church attendance combined with a bit of patriotism. But this lasted only a few months.

However, I am convinced that a major awakening is coming. It will be global, possibly beginning in Britain. The simultaneous combination of the Word and Spirit will cause spontaneous combustion. The realization of death and judgment to follow will at last shake people out of their apathy. A return to a robust faith in the Bible, the preaching of the gospel as taught in Romans 4, and real healings are coming. This awakening will suddenly come and seize the attention of the media and the world in a short period of time.

As in all previous moves of the Spirit since Pentecost, not everyone will be saved. But millions will be saved, including the most surprising conversions. I believe the next great move of God will be led by Africans, African Americans, Hispanics, Koreans, Chinese, university students, and millennials. It will lead to many Muslims coming to Christ. The blindness on many Jews will be lifted. This revival will be devoid of superstars. It will be a simultaneous outbreaking of the fear of the Lord and the joy of the Lord. People will not only believe that Jesus Christ is the only way to God and to heaven; they will believe Jesus is coming soon. Great courage and obedience will be shining evidence of the coming move of the Holy Spirit. Persecution will be as common as people being saved.

God told Joshua in advance that the city of Jericho would be defeated even though it was heavily fortified: "See, I have given Jericho into your hand, with its king and mighty men of valor" (Josh. 6:2). Victory had already taken place, as far as Joshua was concerned. Likewise, Jesus said that whatever you ask for in prayer, "believe that you have received it, and it will be yours" (Mark 11:24). But the children of Israel still had to march around Jericho one time each day for six days and seven times on the seventh day (Josh. 6:3–4) before the walls of Jericho would fall. The children of Israel did precisely that, the walls fell, and they conquered the city in hours (vv. 15–21). The Israelites must have felt like fools as they marched. They looked stupid and silly. But it was what God required—and it worked.

God always requires that those he uses will bear a stigma:

shame and reproach. The stigma is described in one word: embarrassment. Until we are willing to be embarrassed, it is likely that God will not use us.

One Friday afternoon in February 1956, I was driving to my student pastorate in Palmer, Tennessee. Just as I was leaving Nashville, I had an open vision of a blonde girl with long, straight hair wearing a grey and silver robe in a choir. And because this vision came just after I had been jilted by my girlfriend, I was thoroughly convinced that God was forecasting my future wife. I told this vision to dozens and dozens of my friends. In the Trevecca yearbook many wrote, "Hope you get the blonde." I also shared this vision with my dad. I even told it to Dr. William Greathouse, the Dean of Religion at Trevecca Nazarene College. It is impossible to describe the embarrassment I felt years later when I introduced my fiancée, Louise, a brunette with short curly hair, to my dad, not to mention our encounter with Dr. Greathouse during our honeymoon. My greatest fear was that Dr. Greathouse would look flummoxed, and that was exactly the way he appeared when I introduced Louise to him.

I had no choice. I had to introduce Louise, even though it was embarrassing. I got my vision so very, very wrong. You may ask: "Why did you marry Louise and not wait for the blonde to come along?" My simple answer is: because I fell in love with Louise. All the king's horses and all the king's men could not have stopped me from falling in love with her. That was sixty-three years ago. I could never adequately describe what a wonderful wife Louise has been during all this time. By the way, both my dad and Dr. Greathouse were crazy about Louise. I have never doubted that I made the right choice, but neither have I ever doubted having the clear vision of the blonde girl. To this day I believe the vision was from God, but I misinterpreted its purpose for me. One of the purposes, for sure, was to humble me and teach me a hard lesson regarding the mysterious ways and purposes of God. It also shows how what seems to be an obvious interpretation may not be the right interpretation at all!

I share this embarrassing story because I sympathize with those prophets who got it wrong about Donald Trump being reelected on November 3, 2020.

Sooner or later we must choose: Either we can humble ourselves or God will humble us. I am ashamed to say that God has humbled me many more times than I have humbled myself.

True spirituality can be partly understood as closing the time gap between sin and repentance. More precisely, borrowing from the language of Leviticus 6:4, this is a time gap between sinning and *realizing* our guilt. In other words, how long does it take you to admit you sinned? Or made a mistake or got it wrong? Or grieved the Sprit? For some of us, this takes years and years. We may say, "I will *never* admit I was wrong!" and stick to our guns. Others take months before they climb down. Some take weeks, some days, and some hours. Some admit their failures in minutes. And some even repent in seconds!

If we close the time gap to *seconds*, we may get close to knowing God's ways and may have a better sense of how close we are to grieving the Holy Spirit. It is hard for us to perceive that we have grieved the Spirit. For example, when Samson gave Delilah his secret, he didn't feel a thing since he was unaware that the Lord had left him (Judg. 16:20). But we can learn to shorten the time gap between our sin and repentance so that we may *feel* it when we grieve the Spirit. "And do not grieve the Holy Spirit of God, by whom you were sealed for the day of redemption" (Eph. 4:30). The chief way we grieve the Spirit is by *bitterness*—resentment and unwillingness to forgive. This is supported by the very next thing Paul says after warning us not to grieve the Spirit: "Let all bitterness and wrath and anger and clamor and slander be put away from you, along with all malice" (v. 31). Paul then adds: "Be kind to one another, tenderhearted, forgiving one another, as God in Christ forgave you" (v. 32).

One of the most important things I have learned about the ways of God is that he will not bend the rules for *any* of us. For example, God was provoked with ancient Israel because "they have not known my ways" (Heb. 3:10). We all have our ways. You may not like my ways, and I may not like your ways. We may also not like *God's* ways—a more serious matter. The children of Israel did not appear to like God's ways, but Moses's utmost desire was to know these "ways" (Exod. 33:13). The sooner we learn to close the time gap between our mistakes and when we admit them, the more likely we are to know God's ways.

When I preached weekly at Westminster Chapel, I would begin to prepare my sermons on Mondays. I needed six days to be sure my sermon was ready for Sunday morning. Only once in twenty-five years did I wait until Saturday to start preparation for Sunday morning. I had been too busy to prepare earlier during that week. I will never forget the feeling of uneasiness I had on that Saturday morning. I prayed, "Lord, please kindly compensate for my lack of preparation and help me today to get a sermon fit for tomorrow. Let there be no interruptions, no phone calls, and no one knocking at the door." It was 9:00 a.m. All of a sudden, Louise and I got into an argument. In Kentucky, they would call it a "dandy"—it was awful. I thought she was horrible! I slammed the door, went to my desk, and got a blank sheet of paper to write my sermon outline, angrily opening pages in the Bible while praying, "Deal with that woman."

Two hours later the sheet of paper was still blank. I had the Bible opened before me, but no thoughts entered my mind. Not a single thought came. Around 1:00 p.m. I was beginning to learn that God was not going to bend the rules for me just because I was a preacher who was going to preach his Word. At 2:00 p.m. I began to panic. "Lord, please help me. You know that every word I utter tomorrow will go all over the world. You've got to help me." An initial silence from heaven was followed by what seemed to be a rather unsympathetic voice saying, "Really?" Then 4:00 p.m. arrived. (The time gap was now seven hours.) I went into the kitchen and saw Louise standing there in tears.

"Honey, I'm sorry," I began. "It was all my fault."

"It wasn't all your fault," she replied. "It was partly mine."

"No," I insisted. "It was *all* my fault."

We hugged. We kissed. I then went back to that same desk with that same Bible and that same blank sheet of paper. The thoughts began pouring in faster than I could write down. In less than forty-five minutes I had *everything* I needed for the Sunday sermon.

The grieved Holy Spirit became the ungrieved Holy Spirit. My experience shows that we can accomplish more in five minutes when the Holy Spirit comes down than we can in five years if we try to work things up or avoid admitting we got it wrong.

And yet we all hate to admit it when we get it wrong.

The fact is, we all sometimes have gotten it wrong.

God has generally taken his hand off the church—including

off sound evangelicals and sincere charismatics, not to mention the prophetic movement.

As for evangelicals, I will state what I fear about many of them. So many have abandoned their original calling to uphold the gospel: to teach and preach nonstop that God sent his Son into the world to die on a cross for our sins. Our mandate is to preach this gospel and do all we can to save the lost from an eternal hell. Unfortunately, I fear that many have become more churned up over politics than soul winning.

Christians should always hate the things that God hates. We must love people, but we also need to hate the sin they commit. Jesus acknowledged that although the church of Ephesus had abandoned its first love, it still hated certain things that God hated. He commended them: "Yet this you have: you hate the works of the Nicolaitans, which I also hate" (Rev. 2:4–6).

I hope I'm not being unfair, but I sometimes wonder if our hatred for things like abortion and the way biblical marriage is being undermined is how we justify caring more about who is president than winning the lost to Jesus.

Hating things that God hates is not enough. Even though Jesus commended the church of Ephesus for hating what God hates, the saints there were not fully in the right. They still needed to return to "the love [they] had at first" (v. 4). Jesus thus gave the church of Ephesus a wake-up call.

We want traditional American values restored. We want COVID-19 to end. We all want a better quality of life. These are all good things.

Nevertheless, we must also remember that *this life is not all there is*. We are all going to die, and after death comes judgment (Heb. 9:27). *This is why Jesus died.* This is what will ultimately matter to every human being: What happens to us after we die, and where will we spend eternity?

Some important studies have been done regarding the doctrines of grace in the Apostolic Fathers (Christian leaders during the first and second centuries). I was surprised to learn that those people I had admired—and still do, especially since some of them died for the faith—were not known for upholding the gospel of grace which Paul had taught in Romans and Ephesians. I am not saying they did not believe the gospel; of course they did. But if you read what they actually wrote about and what they seem to have regarded as a priority, salvation by grace alone was not what they appeared to talk about. What has been convincingly shown is that the teaching of salvation by grace alone, as taught to the church of Ephesus (see Eph. 2:8–9), fell under a cloud and was upstaged by an emphasis on moralism and good works during the second century. This coheres with Jesus's word to the church at Ephesus in Revelation 2:1–7, which was written just before the beginning of the second century, saying that the saints there had already abandoned their "first love." The first love of the Ephesians had once been the gospel of grace, and every Christian's first love must always be the *gospel*. Good works are important—of course, they are. Godly living is important. The gifts of the Spirit are important. But since God so loved the world that he gave his Son to die for sinners, we should want most of all to see people come to Christ.

I never get tired of repeating it: our first love should always be the gospel and seeing people saved.

Our priorities have been out of focus for too long. "For God so loved the world, that he gave his only Son, that whoever believes in him should not perish but have eternal life" (John 3:16). The mandate from God to the church is to preach the gospel. To reemphasize Arthur Blessitt, the "heartbeat of God" is to see people come to Christ.

Of course, there are Christians that prioritize seeing the lost saved. I thank God for these exceptions. But until the church overwhelmingly returns to our chief mandate, I fear that "Ichabod" might be written over us all: *the glory has departed* (1 Sam. 4:21).

I plead for honesty, however embarrassing it may be for us. I pray for vulnerability. Jesus Christ might have demonstrated his glory and power by avoiding the shame of the cross and raising more Lazaruses from the dead. Not only that, but he could have called tens of thousands of angels to stop the painful ordeal he was about to undergo (Matt. 26:53). But no; he was "crucified in weakness" (2 Cor. 13:4).

By enduring this, Jesus demonstrated great strength.

Repentance—changing our minds and climbing down from refusing to admit that we erred—is something God alone can grant. A study of repentance in the Bible will show that repentance is something God *enables* one to do, not something God is forced to give. When we humbly admit that we got it wrong, God is pleased and honored. Incalculable blessings then follow.

Our attitude should be that of the leper who came to Jesus and said, Lord, "if you will" (as if he was saying, "you don't have to"), "you can make me clean" (Matt. 8:2). We need to ask for mercy. This is only possible when we have nothing to give in exchange. God does not owe us anything. We must never forget this truth: The first thing that the discouraged Hebrew Christians were instructed to ask for was mercy (Heb. 4:16). And because God loves to show mercy, he will grant it to us when we ask humbly.

The call to prophetic integrity is a call to be honest and vulnerable, repenting when you get things wrong. However, if we avoid this honesty, vulnerability, and repentance, revival will be postponed or we may be prevented from seeing the next spiritual awakening.

CONCLUSION

I often say I am too old now to disobey God. Of course, I could still disobey him if I want to be a fool. Even if you are young, you are still too old to disobey God. After all, no matter what our age is, we can still blow it. A lesson to be learned from Shakespeare's *King Lear* is that there is no fool like an old fool. You can be old and be foolish, or you can be young and be wise. You can be old and be tomorrow's man: God did not use Moses until he was eighty (Exod. 7:7). You can be young and be yesterday's man: King Saul was only about forty when God rejected him (1 Sam. 16:1).

Do you want to be a part of the coming spiritual awakening? Here are five ways to know that you qualify to be a part of the next move of the Spirit:

1. If you regard yourself as the most unlikely person God could use, you qualify.
2. If you have been a great sinner but know God's forgiveness through Jesus's blood, you qualify.
3. If virtually nobody knows you, you qualify.

4. If you are not ashamed of the gospel and the blood of
   Jesus, you qualify.
5. If you are willing to be embarrassed before those you
   know and those you don't know, you qualify.

I'm now finished with writing this book.

May the grace of our Lord Jesus Christ, the tender love of
God the Father, and the blessing and sprinkling of Jesus's blood
by the Holy Spirit be yours now and evermore. Amen.